The Year of Grace

The Year of Grace

William Gibson

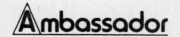

THE YEAR OF GRACE
FIRST PUBLISHED 1860
JUBILEE EDITION 1909
THIS EDITION 1989

COPYRIGHT ©AMBASSADOR PRODUCTIONS LTD. 1989

ISBN 0 907927 33 5

AMBASSADOR PRODUCTIONS LTD.
PROVIDENCE HOUSE
16 HILLVIEW AVENUE
BELFAST BT5 6JR. U.K.

Cover photo 'Belfast 1860' used by permission, The Ulster Museum

PRINTED IN NORTHERN IRELAND BY THE PUBLISHERS

Foreword

It gives me great pleasure to write a foreword to this moving account of the great 1859 Ulster revival by the late Professor William Gibson.

The title of this volume "The Year of Grace" concisely, yet accurately, describes the gracious and glorious happenings in the province during those days of spiritual awakening. 1859 in Ulster was undoubtedly a year of God's grace and that grace was powerfully manifested across the land.

To attribute this blessed spiritual work to any other source than the grace of God would be presumptuous folly. Revival is from God or else it is not true revival. What the Rev. William McCulloch said after the 1742 Cambuslang Revival in Scotland was true of the 1859 Ulster Revival, "It was all of God." Revival is God rending the heavens and coming down. Only God can turn the hearts of 100,000 precious souls to repentance and faith. Only God by His grace can radically change and improve the spiritual, moral and social climate of a community. Only God can restore to a dead and indifferent Church spiritual vitality and Gospel purity and that is exactly what God did in Ulster in 1859. I am strongly of the opinion that God can do this again, but in an age of such spiritual ignorance, theological confusion and human despondency we may first need to recognise once more that revival is a work of God's grace.

With this realisation and prompted by the Spirit of God men became deeply concerned about the spiritual dearth in the Church of their fathers, the moral laxity of society, the lost souls of men, but most of all the glory and honour of God. This concern expresses itself in burdened, passionate, fervent prayer and God responded with a mighty movement of His Spirit upon Ulster.

In his introductory note to the 1909 Jubilee edition of this book, the Right Honourable Thomas Sinclair of Belfast stated that after a lapse of 50 years the events of the revival were almost forgotten history. That statement is not a suggestion that the Ulster Revival of 1859 was not genuine or lasting in its effects, but rather than a generation had been born who had not experienced those days of outpoured blessing on the land. That revival was real and lasting, and every page of this remarkable account by Professor Gibson rings with a sense of reality and authenticity. Every chapter is not only informative, but heart warming and challenging and will stir within the reader a longing that God might revive us again. After 130 years there is a distinct possibility that the great spiritual events of 1859 in Ulster may be forgotten by some and unknown by others, but it is my sincere hope and prayer that the republishing of this wonderful story will bring before this generation the powerful workings of God over a century ago and stimulate in many hearts, especially in those of young people, a desire for such a Divine visitation in our time. Amid the godlessness of this century we desperately need a similar invasion from heaven that will turn the tide of iniquity that is engulfing society and even the Church.

A leading English Christian has stated that hope for revival in England has died in the long waiting and this sentiment may well be applied to most of our nation. May God in His great mercy take this precious record of historic and spiritual fact and use it to restore this hope for a great revival. May the reading of this volume stimulate prevailing prayer for revival and generate revival preaching in the pulpits of the land, in the faith that God may again in providential grace "Rend the heavens and come down" among us once more.

TOM SHAW
Ballycraigy Congregational Church
Newtownabbey

CONTENTS

CHAPTER 1
The Scene of the Revival — page 9

CHAPTER 2
The Birthplace of the Revival — 12

CHAPTER 3
The Revival Proclaimed as Having Come — 22

CHAPTER 4
The Revival in its Development — 29

CHAPTER 5
The Revival in its Progress Northwards — 34

CHAPTER 6
The Revival in Northern Antrim — 49

CHAPTER 7
The Revival in the Capital of Ulster — 66

CHAPTER 8
The Revival Around Belfast — 96

CHAPTER 9
The Revival and the General Assembly — 103

CHAPTER 10
The Revival and the Orangemen — 107

CHAPTER 11
The Revival in County Down — 110

CHAPTER 12
The Revival in County Down - *(continued)* — 124

CHAPTER 13
The Revival in the City and County of Derry — 139

CHAPTER 14
The Revival in County Tyrone — 155

CHAPTER 15
The Revival in County Armagh — 163

CHAPTER 16
The Revival in Donegal, Monaghan, and Cavan — 178

CHAPTER 17
The Revival and the Roman Catholics — 194

CHAPTER 18
The Revival and the Pathological Affections — 216

CHAPTER 19
The Revival and its Lessons — 250

APPENDIX
A-The Revival and Public Morality — 252
B-The Revival and Insanity — 254
C-The Congregational Returns — 256

1

The Scene of the Revival - The Preparation

A HUNDRED years ago the cause of evangelical religion stood very low in Ulster. A general indifference and deadness reigned throughout the Protestant Churches; and the goodly vine which had been planted in the seventeenth century suffered under a withering blight, and was to a lamentable extent shorn of its foliage and fruitfulness. Yet it was not forgotten by the heavenly Husbandman; and now, after having stood the shock of many a tempest, it has been graciously revisited by the genial influences of the Sun of Righteousness, and multitudes are rejoicing in its pleasant fruits.

It is well known that the natives of the north of Ireland bear in their intellectual features the stamp of their Scottish ancestry. Unlike the Milesian Irish of the south and west, they are a shrewd, calculating, and eminently practical people. Superior in education to the generality of their fellow-countrymen, and abjuring the superstitions by which the majority are enslaved, they have ever had a keen appreciation of the strong points of the argument for Protestantism; and as often as a controversial disputation has arisen between the champions of the respective systems, they have looked on with eager interest, and have not failed to honour and reward the victors. The delusions, under the guise of religion, by which the popular mind in England has sometimes been taken captive, had no charm for them—their strong sense and logical discrimination being proof against the impostures of pretenders and the fervours of enthusiasts.

Says the Rev. J. A. Canning of Coleraine:

" In disposition and temperament the people are calm, thoughtful, and far from impulsive, and their habits, amusements, and usages strongly indicate their Scotch descent. Among such a people, thus circumstanced, the *organisation* of Christ's Church has for many years been very complete. Church-courts have been vigilant, ordinances have been regularly and faithfully dispensed, and nothing seemed wanting but *a power* to bring home an offered gospel to the hearts and souls of the people. Some of God's children have therefore been saying of late years that one of two things was likely soon to occur, namely, either that gospel doctrine, preached by ministers and professed by the people, but apparently without much life, would, like everything which becomes stagnant, sink into putrefaction, and that heresy would supplant the truth; or, that a gracious God would honour His own truth by supplying the power of the Spirit to impart to it a vivifying energy. That God has been pleased to shed abroad this power the wondrous awakening which has characterised the history of the summer and autumn of 1859 abundantly proves."

" It is right it should be known," says the Rev. S. M. Dill of Ballymena,[1] " that this movement has not come upon us so suddenly as people at a distance might suppose. There has been a gradual but perceptible improvement in the state of religion throughout this

[1] Afterwards Professor of Theology in Magee College, Londonderry.

SCENE OF THE REVIVAL—PREPARATION

district for some years. Ministers were led to speak to the people with greater earnestness about 'the things which belong to their peace.' Attendance on the public ordinances of religion had considerably increased. Open-air preaching was extensively practised. Sabbath-schools were greatly multiplied. Prayer-meetings were growing up in many districts. Sacred music, which had been much neglected, was cultivated with ardour and success. And altogether the people were in a state of preparation—a state which passed into one of earnest expectancy, when the glad news of the American revival reached our shores."

2

The Birthplace of the Revival

IN more than one locality in Ulster, notwithstanding the general deadness, symptoms of awakening began to indicate the approach of a better era. Public attention, however, was soon concentrated on a rural district in County Antrim, which more than any other has been identified with the early history of the movement, and from which, as a common centre, it spread with unprecedented rapidity over the entire north of Ireland.

The place was one which had long enjoyed the benefit of an evangelical ministry. Even in days of darkness and defection Connor had been a favoured district; and under the oversight of a faithful pastorate and vigilant eldership, zealous for the purity of communion and the maintenance of a wholesome discipline, the flock were taught alike by precept and example the necessity of separation from the world. Some eighty years ago the venerable Henry Henry rested from his labours, extending over half a century, and was succeeded by one who, in the wider sphere to which he was subsequently called, acquired an influential position in the Presbyterian Church. For about nine years the Rev. David Hamilton, late of Belfast, plied his congenial task among a plain people in that rural region, and sowed much of that precious seed which has subsequently borne abundant fruit. His successor, one of the ablest and most devoted ministers in Ulster, laboured for a length

THE BIRTHPLACE OF THE REVIVAL

of time with little visible result, expounding and enforcing the old theology, training the rising generation in Scripture knowledge, using no flattering words with any, and fearing not to testify of the dread realities of the world to come.

In the spring of 1855 a movement was commenced in faith and prayer, which was destined erelong to spread over the neighbourhood a hallowed influence. At the close of a Sabbath evening at that period, at one of his Bible-class examinations Mr Moore addressed a young man present, and affectionately urged upon him the duty of doing "something more" for God. "Could you not," he said, "gather at least six of your careless neighbours, either parents or children, to your own house or some other convenient place, on the Sabbath, and spend an hour with them, reading and searching the Word of God?" The young man hesitated for a moment, but promised to try. From that trial, made in faith, originated the Tannybrake Sabbath-school, and in connection with it, two years subsequently, a prayer-meeting, which yielded some of the first-fruits of the great awakening. In the course of the winter following, a devoted Christian layman came to reside in the vicinity, with whose co-operation, in the spring, the school, which had been closed during the months preceding, was reopened under more favourable auspices. During the summer it greatly flourished, a marked seriousness and earnestness being discernible both among the teachers and the taught. Seeing the good effects produced upon the children, the teachers anxiously considered whether an effort might not be undertaken on behalf of the parents also. Accordingly they resolved to commence a special meeting for prayer and reading the Scriptures each evening, after the closing of the school, to which the parents and others were to be specially invited. "One Sabbath evening early in August," to use the language of a student for the ministry residing in the district, "found the expectant teachers engaged in their new work, *with only one solitary visitor present*. Nothing discouraged, they resolved to persevere, and a second meeting showed a more decided measure of success, for about thirty persons, besides themselves and a few scholars, attended. From week to week the numbers continued to increase, till at last the house was filled. Prayer, praise, and reading of the Bible, with plain observations on the portion read, were the exercises engaged in. Everything sectarian was strictly prohibited, and promptly checked as soon as it appeared. Questions that might have given rise to controversy were not discussed, while the one great and absorbing topic, 'Christ and the Cross,' seemed to occupy the attention and steal the affections of all present. The Sabbath-school teachers' prayer-meeting, for so it was called, became more and more interesting, till the knowledge of its existence spread throughout the neighbourhood.

"Among others who were associated in the Sabbath-school prayer-meeting, were four young men whose names have been much before the public in connection with the subsequent revival. These four rejoiced together in the glorious work, and took great delight also in each other's society, enjoying sweet communion with each other and with their common Lord. But as they lived some miles apart, and could not come together so often as they desired, they resolved to meet at a central place for Christian fellowship, and for this purpose they chose an old school-house in the neighbourhood of Kells, where, in the month of October, about two months

THE BIRTHPLACE OF THE REVIVAL

subsequent to the commencement of the Sabbath-school prayer-meeting in Tannybrake, those exercises were conducted which have been generally regarded as the origin of the revival. It will be seen, however, from what has now been stated, that the first stirrings of life were exhibited in connection with the Sabbath-school prayer-meeting. Three, at least, of the converts were born there; two of them were scholars, and the third a teacher, while the gracious answers to the prayers offered on their behalf gave a powerful stimulus to prayer itself. From that time the gracious drops began to fall thicker and faster, until the rushing shower descended which has refreshed so many, and left behind verdure and beauty in the heritage of God."

"For a considerable period," Mr Moore adds, "before any general interest in religion was manifested by the people, there had been a growing anxiety about salvation. And some cases had here and there occurred of an unwonted character: a sinner, anxious about the state and prospects of his soul, experiencing a sudden, startling visitation of dread, followed by a peace and joy unspeakable—a protracted season of perplexity approaching to despair, succeeded by a view of Christ as a Saviour, full, sweet, restoring. About the spring of 1858 a very interesting work began to manifest itself, and to move onwards over a certain district of the congregation. For more than a quarter of a century the 'prayer-meeting' had existed in that locality, while similar meetings had in other districts, after many ineffectual efforts to maintain them, languished and revived, languished again, and died. Once the meeting in question was so far reduced in numbers that only two came together to call upon the name of the Lord. Still they continued to pray on, and by degrees the little company increased until it became 'two bands.' In the same district, also, the Bible training of the young in connection with the organisation of Sabbath-schools had been most successful; the class which had been established there being more promising than any of the others in the parish."

The "fellowship-meeting" above referred to, was established almost simultaneously with those concerts for prayer begun by a similar agency in America, whose influence was so extensively felt throughout the great Western continent. "The society," to adopt the words of the Rev. S. J. Moore of Ballymena, "soon ceased to be a secret one; and slowly one kindred spirit after another was introduced on the recommendation of some of the original members. For a few months they had to walk by faith, but the seed was not long cast upon the waters till the tender blade sprung up. The first observable instance of conversion occurred in December following. A young man became greatly alarmed. After some time, in answer to earnest prayer by himself and others, he found peace and confidence. Early in January a youth in the Sabbath-school class taught by one of those young men was brought to the saving knowledge of Christ as his Saviour. Special prayer about the same period was frequently offered in the fellowship-meeting in behalf of two persons, who some three months afterwards joyfully professed their faith in the Lord Jesus. Faith grew. Hope brightened. 'The power of prayer' began to be known and felt and seen. The spring communion came on. Throughout the extensive parish, consisting of some thousand families, it was generally known that lately persons had been turned to the Lord among them, some moral, and some wildly immoral. The services were peculiarly solemn. The Master's presence seemed to be recognised, and His call heard. The old prayer-

THE BIRTHPLACE OF THE REVIVAL 17

meetings began to be thronged, and many new ones established. No difficulty now to find persons to take part in them. Humble, grateful, loving, joyous converts multiplied. The awakening to a sight of sin, the conviction of its sinfulness, the illumination of the soul in the knowledge of a glorious Saviour, and conversion to Him—all this operation, carried on by the life-giving Spirit, was in the Connor district for more than eighteen months a calm, quiet, gradual, in some cases a lengthened process, not commencing in, or accompanied by, any extraordinary physical effects, more than what might be expected to result from great anxiety and deep sorrow."

It is a striking fact that it was not till more than twelve months subsequently, in the summer of 1859, when the work was spreading generally over Ulster, that some of the other districts of the congregation were blessed with the gracious visitation. Once begun, however, the movement rapidly extended. The great concerns of eternity were realised as they had never been before. People, when they met, talked a new language. Many walked about in anxiety about the one thing needful, while others rejoiced in the realised experience of a present peace and a complete salvation. Meetings for Christian converse and prayer began to spread; in a short time the community was altogether changed in its outward aspects, and a pervading seriousness pervailed; and at the meeting of the General Assembly in July 1858, Mr Moore was publicly requested by the Moderator to furnish some account of the awakening, the tidings of which elicited an expression of the deepest interest on the part of the supreme judicatory of the Presbyterian Church.

During the succeeding months and throughout the winter a silent work of grace was gradually extending over the whole congregation of Connor, insomuch that when spring arrived it was believed that some hundreds had been savingly brought under its benign influence. As yet no physical excitement had appeared ; the process was a purely spiritual one, carried on in the sanctuary of the mind—the Spirit of God acting through the medium of His own truth upon the spirit of man. Conversion-work, however, of the purest type had been going on ; a total transformation had been effected in the hearts and lives of those who were the subjects of the change ; and throughout all the neighbourhood was heard "thanksgiving and the voice of melody."

It was early in the month of May 1859, that, having heard of the great events that were being transacted there, I resolved to make a personal visit to the scene. Arriving on a Saturday afternoon at the manse, I found my excellent friend the pastor in the bosom of his family ; his mind, which had for such a lengthened period previously been strained to the utmost, now somewhat relaxed into repose, as he was relieved for the time from preparation for the public services of the morrow. I had not long arrived till an intimation was sent from the neighbouring village, from a little company of praying ones, whose custom it was to meet on the evening before the Sabbath to invoke a blessing on the ministrations of the sanctuary. The place of meeting was the same which on a subsequent occasion was visited by the Rev. Dr Edgar, and was thus graphically described by him : " It was a butcher's shop. The butcher two years ago did not know A from B. God converted him : he taught himself to read, and he is now a large tract-distributor at his own cost, and a chief hand in the revival work. The secretary was a working shoemaker—another Carey. Others present were day-labourers, a stone-breaker, and a blacksmith's boy. The stonebreaker, who sits on the road-side breaking

THE BIRTHPLACE OF THE REVIVAL

stones to earn his bread, is one of four brothers, lately converted. Their mother was sister of a notorious pugilist, to whom she used to be a bottle-holder, and when she entered a shop she was watched as a noted thief. Her sons were pests, but God's grace has made them vessels of mercy, overflowing with goodness for not a few."

The services on the Sabbath were attended as usual by an immense audience. The congregation being one of the largest in Ulster, comprising nearly a thousand families, the church, at all times well filled, was thronged by a mass of devout worshippers. During the service there were indications of an unusual solemnity, the most intense earnestness being depicted on every countenance, and many being melted into tears. The singing of the psalms was a perfect outburst of melodious sound, the greater portion of the people having for some years previously been trained in the practice of sacred music, and their hearts being manifestly engaged in the enlivening exercise. When the service, which had been somewhat more protracted than usual, concluded, the pastor requested as many as could find it convenient to remain for an additional half hour, for the purpose of invoking the Divine blessing on the statements which they had then heard. The greater portion of the audience remained, when, after a brief exposition of a psalm, a request was made that some member of the church would engage in supplication. The call was at once responded to, and our devotions were led with much appropriateness by an individual who, as his pastor afterwards informed me, had not on any former occasion taken such a part in the public services of the house of God.

In the evening of that Sabbath I took the opportunity of visiting one of the many meetings for exhortation and prayer in the vicinity, selecting that (as being nearest) in the adjacent village of Kells. The exercises had begun and were going forward when we entered. The house in which the meeting was held was filled to inconvenience, the greater portion occupying the available space above, while the ground floor was crowded, and the very stair was occupied in every part. There was the utmost order and decorum, and for some twenty minutes we sat listening with much interest, unobserved by the speaker, who was overhead, to a very touching address delivered by one of comparatively tender years, in which he dwelt with pathetic earnestness on the necessity of an instant closing with Christ on His own terms, as the only and all-sufficient Saviour. After he had concluded, and prayer had been engaged in, it was agreed that, in consequence of the crowded and uncomfortable condition of the apartments, an adjournment should take place to another house hard by; which being done, the exercises were resumed — Mr Moore himself presiding. There were many present who appeared to be in deep mental concern. It was now nine o'clock, and we took our leave, the benediction having been pronounced. We left the majority, however, still in a state of apparent expectation, and showing, from the way in which they lingered outside, a disposition to engage once more in exercises which were manifestly so much in unison with their feelings. I have little doubt that they did resume in the same place the congenial occupation.

A short time after we had returned to the pastor's dwelling, an intimation was made to us that in the course of the morning service a young man who had for some time been under anxiety of mind had obtained " peace in believing "; —" but that," said my excellent brother, " is nothing uncommon, for scarce a sermon is preached or meeting held in which some such results are not realised."

THE BIRTHPLACE OF THE REVIVAL

Next morning I took my departure. On passing through the village, Mr Moore alighted from the vehicle on which we were conveyed, and entered a respectable-looking dwelling. On his rejoining me, he said, " Yes, it is even as we heard last night. That is a house which is visited by almost all our younger converts as soon as they have obtained peace. They are all in Christ in that habitation, and there others are attracted by the assurance of their sympathy. Late in the evening, the young man referred to, a holder of land in the neighbourhood, had called. He told them that at such a part of the service his burden was lifted off, and when he came to them, as they expressed it, " the tears were trickling down his cheeks for very joy."

Continuing our drive, we passed two houses by the wayside, referring to which my friend said, as he pointed to them, " There are seven in that little nook," meaning thereby that these had also through grace believed. Had time and opportunity allowed me to accompany Mr Moore in some of his pastoral rounds, I have little doubt that he could have pointed out hundreds of such cases.

In regard to the results of the revival, as witnessed in the improved state of the district, one or two statistical facts may be mentioned. Of nine public-houses, two are closed by the conversion of their owners, and a third for want of trade ; while the quantity of drink now sold by the six that are open is less than that formerly sold by one. In 1857 there were in the parish thirty-seven committals for offences connected with drunkenness ; in 1858, eleven ; in 1859, four, of whom two were strangers. And whereas in 1857 there were twenty-seven paupers in the Union Workhouse, there are now but four, while the poor-rates are only half the amount they were before.

3

The Revival Proclaimed as Having Come

ALTHOUGH, as has been already stated, the work of preparation was going forward in some of the neighbouring congregations, it was not till near the close of 1858 that any striking results appeared. On the 9th of December that year, an event occurred which was destined to exert a widespread spiritual influence. On that day a young man who had been led to attend the Connor fellowship-meeting was for the first time penetrated with a sense of sin and induced to cry for mercy. No sooner had he tasted the joys of pardon and of peace than he began to bethink himself of the state of his relations, resident a few miles off, in the Ahoghill district; and with all the fervour of a young disciple he solicited some three or four of his fellow-converts to unite with him in prayer on their behalf, that they also might be made partakers of his abounding happiness. A few weeks after, he visited his mother and family, to communicate to them his own experience of the loving-kindness of the Lord, and to excite them to a kindred earnestness about the " great salvation." Once and again he came with the same anxious and prayerful aim; nor was it long till he was gladdened by the tidings that, after an exercise of conviction, his mother had been made a partaker of like precious faith, and was rejoicing in the hope of glory. Another member of the family, a brother, was the next object of his solicitude. At the time when he went in

THE REVIVAL PROCLAIMED

search of him, the brother was at a shooting match, and there, amid the excitement of the scene, fell on his ear the startling words, "I have a message for you from the Lord Jesus." A strange effect soon followed, and he was brought under the subduing influence of a Divine agency. It was amid the clouds of night that after parting from one another the brother resident at Ahoghill was all at once immersed in the horror of a deeper darkness, his whole frame trembling as in the immediate presence of the Invisible. In the midst of a soul-conflict, in which he experienced the pangs of unutterable agony, he found a measure of relief in prostrating himself before the throne of mercy, and though still much agitated and enfeebled, made the best of his way home. Day after day he groaned under the weight of his heart-sorrow, and sought deliverance with awful cries and supplications. At length his burden was graciously removed, and, rising from his loom, he fell upon his knees, and gave full vent to his rejoicing in rapturous thanksgivings. Thenceforward a new life was infused into him, and he burned with an unquenchable desire to glorify the name of his Almighty Saviour. One of his first impulses was to rush directly to his minister (the Rev. F. Buick), to whom he communicated his whole soul in the glad utterance, "I am saved." And then, as he found opportunity, he wrought unceasingly both night and day, and even to the neglect of his daily task, in seeking to win others to a participation in the same immortal hope. In a short time several members of the same household experienced a gracious change.

An anxious desire having been expressed by Mr Buick that others of the lay brethren from Connor should visit the neighbourhood, a meeting was held in his own church, to which they were invited. "It was," as he testifies, "an earnest, heart-stirring meeting. A holy flame was kindled. A strong desire for a gracious revival began to gain ascendancy. The brethren from Connor were again invited. The house-school, where the meeting was to be held, was altogether too small to accommodate the hundreds that were in attendance. It was accordingly adjourned to the Second Presbyterian Church, Ahoghill, where similar stirring appeals and prayers of burning fervency moved the vast assembly. Thereafter, prayer-meetings began to multiply. The new converts, with other Christians whose hearts the Lord stirred, engaged in the work of prayer and exhortation with unquenchable zeal. Thus the work spread, fresh interest being daily awakened. Common houses, and even large churches, were not able to contain the multitudes that assembled, so that often the highway and the open field, in the cold evenings of spring, were the scenes of deeply-interesting meetings. So eager were the multitudes to hear the services of the converted brethren that many travelled miles to be present, and, without any weariness, they would have remained even all night, if the services had continued. There was an uncommon thirsting for the Word."

In the statements which follow, the physical affections which henceforward characterised the movement are thus noticed in their early manifestations:—

"At these meetings many convictions have taken place. From one up to ten and twelve have been arrested by the Spirit of God through the word and prayer of these honoured brethren. Even strong men have staggered and fallen down under the wounds of their conscience. Great bodily weakness ensues. The whole frame trembles. Oh! it is a heartrendiing sight to witness. With wringing of hands, streams of tears, and a look of unutterable anguish, they confess their sins in tones of unmistakable sincerity, and appeal to the Lord for mercy with a cry of piercing earnestness. I have seen the strong frame canvulsed; I have witnessed every joint trembling; I have heard the cry as I have never heard it before, ' Lord Jesus, have mercy upon my sinful soul; Lord Jesus, come to my burning heart; Lord, pardon my sins; oh, come and lift me from these flames of hell!'

"These convictions vary in different individuals, both in strength and duration. While some obtain peace in believing soon after their conviction, others do not attain it for several days. It is after many a conflict, with conviction oft returning, with much prayer and reading of the Word, through which spiritual light makes great progress in the mind, that a settled peace and holy joy take possession of the soul."

While the bodily prostrations above referred to have been generally regarded as originating in connection with the awakening in Ahoghill, there is reason to believe there were occasional instances of a similar description, and at the same period, in other parts of Ulster. Thus, in the county of Down, in a rural district called Crossgar, the following case is narrated by the Rev. J. G. Thomson, the young minister of the place:—

"In the middle of the month of January 1859, I was called upon early one morning to see a previously strong, healthy young man, who supposed himself to be dying. On my arrival, I found him lying in bed, and evidently in a state of great bodily weakness, although his sickness did not seem to be unto death. Entering into conversation with him, I learned that he had been sick of soul previous to his being sick of body, and that the former was the cause of the latter. He told me that he had been very much impressed by a sermon I had preached on the last Sabbath afternoon, from these words, "I have a message from God unto thee." (Judges iii. 20.) Alarmed on account of sin and the punishment due to it, he could get no rest day or night. Loudly did he cry for mercy, and did not cry in vain. He obtained pardon and peace after a severe struggle, by which he was left in a state of great bodily weakness. He was unable to walk for a number of days, and not until two months had passed was he able to pursue his ordinary business. Strange to say, when affected first, he complained of there being about his heart, unattended by any pain, a heavy weight, which he considered in some way to be associated with the idea of sin. This was removed, as he said, when the Holy Spirit came into his heart, and produced within him that faith which enabled him to lay hold upon Jesus, and to fly to Him from the wrath to come. His features indicated the gladness of one who had found some great and lasting treasure. You could have seen the very joy sparkling in his eye; and more than once did I hear him say that, if the Lord willed, he would rather depart and be with Jesus. His case was, in many particulars, similar to that of many I have seen since the great religious movement came among us. While his weakness remained, I frequently read the Scriptures, conversed and prayed with him. In all such exercises, he took, and still takes, the deepest interest. He is still growing in grace, and by his walk and conversation in the world gives every evidence of being a son of the Lord Almighty. This and similar cases have been like drops before the shower."

Many interesting incidents might be narrated, illustrative of the wonderful effect which was produced upon the public mind. Take the following as an instance, narrated by the Rev. David Adams :—

THE REVIVAL PROCLAIMED

"I may quote a statement respecting a meeting at Creaghrock, midway between Ahoghill and Randalstown, a place where ever since, at the request of the people, a monthly religious meeting has been held in the open-air, attended by hundreds. This place has become famous, or rather infamous, as a cockpit, especially on Ahoghill old fairday, when thousands would assemble for the degrading sport of cock-fighting, thereby making it a scene of lying, blasphemy, drunkenness, and all manner of profligacy. In these ' revival ' times a number of the awakened, some of whom, perhaps, were ' cockers ' themselves, resolved on this occasion to make it a far different scene, and therefore invited several ministers to attend, and address the meeting against all manner of vice, and for the promotion of all manner of holiness. The meeting was at ten o'clock A.M., and even at that early hour, crowds in all directions, and of all characters —in many cases from a distance of five or six miles— were seen wending their way gladly to the Rock, and at one time there could not have been much less than two thousand present. The meeting was addressed by four ministers, and pious prayers were offered up by fervent laymen. A most solemn impression was produced on all, from the grey-haired man of ninety to the merry child of a few years, and many of the old and young were deeply and visibly impressed by the Spirit's power."

A twelvemonth has elapsed since the blessing came upon the neighbourhood of which such things have been recorded. Have the results disappointed expectation ? or has the impression died away with the occasion that gave it birth ? Let the following statement, written at the close of the past year, supply the answer. It is by the Rev. F. Buick :—

"The grace of God is visible in its effects in producing

light and knowledge, prayer and praise, attendance on ordinances, holiness of life, and reformation of manners. Great gladness has been obtained by hundreds who have come to the enjoyment of pardon and peace, and are now rejoicing in the Lord. Great gladness has been introduced into families. Men that were coarse and savage, and a source of untold misery to their wives, are now so altered, so mild, so pleasant, so God-like, that the change in their domestic happiness is like heaven on the earth. There is great gladness in the Church because of the increased attendance in the courts of the Lord's house, the lofty strains of her praise, the deep-toned earnestness of her services, and the life and power of her devotions.

"It is the general impression that a work of grace has been going on silently, and without observation, on the heart of hundreds throughout the country, who have had no bodily prostrations. It is known by the feeling of deep solemnity that pervades the neighbourhood—by the vast increase of family religion— by the absence of hitherto prevailing sins—by the keeping up of prayer-meetings in almost every locality—by the great increase in the attendance on the ordinances of God's house—and by the large accessions which have been made to the communicants' roll in all the churches. The three Presbyterian churches in Ahoghill are full; and the Second and Third are contemplating large additions to their accommodation."

4

The Revival in its Development

BALLYMENA is three miles distant from Ahoghill. It is one of the most flourishing inland towns in Ulster, with a population of about 6000 and a principal seat of the linen trade. Here fifty years ago the work began early in April.

I shall narrate its progress in the words of a young friend who took part in the movement in his native town :—

"The week which began with May 17th can never be forgotten, though it cannot easily be described. When the great outpouring came, worldly men were silent with an indefinite fear, and Christians found themselves borne onward in the current, with scarce time for any feeling but the outpouring conviction that a great revival had come at last. Careless men were bowed in unaffected earnestness, and sobbed like children. Drunkards and boasting blasphemers were awed into solemnity and silence. Sabbath-school teachers and scholars became seekers of Christ together ; and languid believers were stirred up to unusual exertion. There was great earnestness with all, and enthusiasm with some, but little extravagance or ridicule was known. Ministers who had often toiled in heartless sorrow suddenly found themselves beset by inquirers, and wholly unequal to the demands which were made. Every day many were hopefully converted : passing through an ordeal of conviction more or less severe, to realise their great deliverance, and to throw themselves with every energy into the work of warning others, or of leading them to the Lord.

"All this came suddenly, and many thought it strange. It was little marvel that the world was astonished, but the incredulous wonder of many Christians shewed how much we needed a revival. We were astonished that God took us at our word, and sent at last the quickening grace for which we had been dreamily praying so long. The theory of asking and receiving was common, but the getting of a blessing for which there was no room was rare. 'Thy kingdom come' was familiar; but the coming kingdom was the wonder of the day.

"It was in the opening summer that the revival came, when the daylight lingers so long, and the bright morning break so soon. We can remember how many lighted windows there were though the night was far gone, and how prayer-meetings were prolonged till the day had returned again. Every evening the churches were crowded, and family worship became almost universal. In the country large meetings were held in the open air, and hundreds were often visibly impressed by strong conviction. Part of the dinner hour was generally devoted to singing and prayer, and the sound from numerous groups of worshippers could be heard afar borne on the summer breeze. Thousands of tracts were circulated and read with avidity, and long-neglected Bibles came into general use. The order of an accustomed formality was gone; and while exhausted ministers were compelled to leave the meetings, the people reluctantly dispersed—some to pray over unimpressed friends, others to feel the workings of an awakened conscience, and many to rejoice in their new liberty, and to glory in their King.

THE REVIVAL IN ITS DEVELOPMENT

"The order of procedure at the town meetings was little varied, yet the interest never failed while the summer lasted. Each evening had its own incidents, but one general sketch may give an idea of all.

"For some time before the appointed hour, many of the younger converts assemble to sing together some favourite hymns. A little later the people pour in rapidly and soon every seat is occupied, men of business sitting beside their workers, all in their usual attire. A large proportion is made up of the scholars in the Sabbath-school and of the lower classes, who were specially visited during the awakening. Some seem very anxious, and all are solemn. On the faces of the recent converts there is such a beaming gladness that even a stranger can tell their story at a look.

"A few minutes after the single stroke of the hour is heard, the minister ascends the pulpit stairs, and reads the opening psalm, which is sung with thrilling fervency. The prayer which follows bears greatly on the three classes of worshippers, the converted, the anxious and the unawakened, and contains earnest pleadings for the Spirit's presence and for the spread of the revival work. Very often as the petition passes, there is heard, far above the speaker's voice the thrilling cry of some who were arrested as they prayed. And as many a conscience trembles at the arousing call, others silently offer a prayer to the Great Physician of souls, that the broken-hearted penitent may enjoy the healing of His grace.

"The addresses which follow from <u>lay members or others</u> are practical and earnest. The master-truths pressed home are the guilt and danger of every unconverted listener, and the full and present salvation of Jesus. Recent incidents are quoted, and each is brought to bear on the pressing appeal. At the close, the leader usually gives a short summary of the revival progress in the surrounding districts, and then reads the first line of the favourite hymn, ' What's the News ? ' Then follows the closing prayer, and the benediction. On several occasions this had to be pronounced twice, and, though at midnight, all had not dispersed.

"Experiences have varied greatly. Some have escaped so gently that they scarcely knew when their chains fell, and the freedom came. Others have writhed and struggled in their bonds so long that reason almost sank in the strife. We have heard of some who wandered about in morbid gloominess for months, while on a brother or sister the light has broken in a day. One can tell how he has hardly been saved from his diabolical enemy, whom a racked imagination made almost visible ; and another can speak of nothing but the story of a wondrous Deliverer, and how He brought light and liberty to the darkened soul. When the mind has been stored by previous training, there is needed only the quickening life ; but when conviction of peril finds no trust to fall back upon, there is a fearful groping in darkness and in doubt. This brings us many lessons in reference to the early teaching of the elements of truth. These life-seeds cannot perish ; they lie till the life swells them, and the spring-time of the soul comes round. ' God's Word,' says Samuel Rutherford, ' will come to God's harvest.' The psalms and lessons of the Sabbath-class have been reproduced so clearly that many thought the revival miraculous. A minister was astonished to hear a woman of his charge, who had been convicted, repeat with great feeling and striking accuracy the instructions of a communion class at which he had laboured about thirty years before. This quickening of the memory brings back the truth, when every nerve is strained in the grasping after

THE REVIVAL IN ITS DEVELOPMENT

safety, and fits workers for their duty when the need is felt.

"Another lesson may be inserted here. It is the power of urgent, personal dealing. We who work for the Master are too slack and listless with perishing men.

"As the work progressed, every rank felt its power, and shared in its good fruits. The labouring classes were first and largely impressed; but the awakening seemed as great among the rich and respectable. Among the young there has been a decided and special quickening. In a denominational point of view, no Church has been so favoured as the Calvinistic Presbyterian, though sectarian differences have been greatly overlooked. Many Unitarians and Roman Catholics were convinced of their errors, and hopefully changed. It would be untrue, on the one hand, to describe the sudden and complete check which was given to current vice as a lasting change; and unjust, on the other, to consider the reflux of the interrupted current as an evidence of universal defection. Deep, real, enduring the work has been. A few abuses we admit, but unnumbered blessings we maintain. Christ's credit is in it, and He will guard His own."

5
The Revival in its Progress Northwards

WITHIN about three miles of Ballymena stands the village of Broughshane, the centre of a densely-inhabited and almost exclusively Presbyterian district. At an early period the awakening spread in that direction. One morning a number of young women were affected in a spinning factory hard by. Immediately intense excitement spread among the workers, and within an hour twenty or thirty persons of both sexes were laid prostrate. The business of the entire establishment was interrupted, and, as a matter of necessity, it was closed. When re-opened two days after, nearly half the usual hands were absent. About the same time a congregation of several thousands assembled in the open air in front of the Presbyterian church, and the services were not concluded till an advanced period of the evening. In the village itself and all the country round such meetings were of frequent occurrence throughout the summer months, and hundreds, there is reason to believe, were brought in connection with them under the power of a Divine influence.

A visitor, at the beginning of the awakening, thus describes the presence and address of a Brougshane convert at a meeting in a quarry pit, at which there were several thousands in attendance :—

" Near the end of the preaching one old man stood up to address the multitude. He was a remarkable-looking man. I was beside him before he rose. A dealer in rags would not have given more than sixpence for all the clothes he had on his person. He bore the marks and tokens of a 'hard liver,' a confirmed drunkard. He spoke something to the following effect, as nearly as I can remember:—' Gentlemen,' and he trembled as he spoke —' gentlemen, I appear before you this day as a vile sinner. Many of you know me; you have but to look at me, and recognise the profligate of Broughshane. You know I was an old man, hardened in sin; you know I was a servant of the devil, and he led me by that instrument of his, the spirit of the barley. I brought my wife and family to beggary more than fifty years ago; in short, I defy the townland of Broughshane to produce my equal in profligacy or any sin whatever. But, ah, gentlemen, I have seen Jesus; I was born again on last night week; I am, therefore, a week old to-day, or about. My heavy and enormous sin is all gone; the Lord Jesus took it away; and I stand before you this day, not only a pattern of profligacy, but a monument of the perfect grace of God! I stand here to tell you that God's work on Calvary is perfect; yes, I have proved it, His work is perfect. Had it not been so, it would have been capable of reaching the depths of iniquity of——, the profligate nailer of Broughshane.' "

The following statement dated 26th April 1860, by the Rev. Archibald Robinson, of Broughshane, sets forth the character and progress of the work in that important district.

The First Case.—" The first case of awakening here was of a very peculiar and solemn kind. It was in 1858. It was that of a man who had been a drunkard. He was drunk the week before. In the middle of the night he awoke and roused the family out of their beds—said he had had a dream—an angel came and told him to be up and busy praying for mercy, for he would die at one o'clock, or, if not at one, decidedly at four o'clock next day. He dressed, and gave himself up entirely to reading and prayer. People thought he was mad—in *delirium tremens*. He refused all solicitations to induce him to drink—went about wringing his hands and entreating mercy, till about one o'clock—went to his bed, and died happy about four!

The Full Outpouring.—" It was not, however, till May 1859 that we were visited with a most gracious and abundant outpouring of the Holy Spirit. We had been praying for and expecting some such precious blessing, but were, notwithstanding, taken by surprise, so sudden, powerful, and extraordinary were the manifestations of the Spirit's presence. Persons of every shade of temperament and character were mysteriously affected, overpowered, prostrated, and made to pour out the most thrilling agonising cries for mercy. Most of those thus impressed and awakened found peace and comfort in a very short time, and then their countenances shone with a sweetness and glory beyond description. Very many of them received a marvellous fluency and power of prayer. A hatred of sin, a love for the Saviour, a zeal for His cause, an affection for one another, and an anxiety about perishing sinners, took possession of their hearts, and literally ruled and governed their actions. For about six weeks almost all agricultural operations, and indeed every kind of secular employment, were suspended, no man being able to think of or attend to anything but the interests of his soul. Night and day the sound of praise and prayer never ceased to float upon the air. An overwhelming sense of awe and terror held in check the boldest sinners, while thousands who till now had lived as if eternity were a priestly fiction seemed for the first time to realise its truth and presence, and to feel as if the end of all things was at hand. I should say about one thousand people were suddenly, sensibly, and powerfully impressed and awakened. Fully one half of this number, if not more, have profited by their experience, and are as fair and hopeful cases of conversion as one could well desire, while not less than five hundred were silently, gradually, and without observation brought, I may say, from death unto life, or from a state of stupor and coldness into a state of activity and warmth, and are now rejoicing in the peace that passeth understanding. Not less than twenty Roman Catholics came under the power of the truth, and were made to acknowledge the errors of the Church of Rome. Three of these were rebaptized at their own urgent request, and afterwards admitted to the Lord's Supper. The others still attend the prayer-meetings, and now and again the public worship of the sanctuary.

The Praying Matrons.—" In one district of country almost all the matrons within an area of more than two miles were graciously visited and converted in the most satisfactory and conclusive manner, if we can so speak about another's conversion at all. These women have exercised a mighty influence on their families and neighbourhood ; and if one wishes to see the religion of the Cross in its loveliest features, in the simplicity, beauty, and power of primitive times, he has but to pay this district a visit and see and hear for himself. I have no doubt he will return, saying that the half has not been told him.

" The gift of prayer bestowed on these matrons is beyond conception, and certainly it is not left to rust. They have a prayer-meeting of their own—none but females being admitted—the exercises of which are praise, prayer, and reading the Scriptures without note or comment. This meeting has tended greatly to fan the flame of love in their own hearts, and kindle it in others who come. We have many such female prayer-meetings, and I am satisfied of their utility.

"About the month of August the physical features of the revival in a great measure passed away, but we had abundant evidence that the work of the Lord was still going on, more silently but as progressively as ever. The Holy Ghost, we rejoice to say, has not been as a wayfaring man with us. His gracious operations have not as yet ceased. From time to time we have been constrained to note unmistakable signs of His presence and power. Seldom does a week elapse without some groping, hoping, praying soul finding Christ, pardon, and peace in a way more or less marked and visible. Frequently our prayer-meetings have experienced a sudden, mysterious, overpowering impulse, swaying the whole assembly as one man, and leaving all weeping, praying, rejoicing. Men have felt as if the Lord had breathed upon them. They were first affected with awe and fear—then they were bathed in tears—then filled with love unspeakable. Such a scene as this occurred about a month ago in the midst of the ordinary services of the Sabbath.

General Results.—"True and undefiled religion has received a mighty impetus here. Since May 1859 it has been progressing in the most satisfactory and cheering manner. Never in the experience of the oldest members of our church were the spiritual interests of the people of this parish so far advanced and so promising. Without any fear of exaggeration or disappointment I may say we can count true and decided cases of conversion, not by tens, not by fifties, but by hundreds. The house of God

REVIVAL IN ITS PROGRESS NORTHWARDS 39

is filled Sabbath after Sabbath by an overflowing congregation of anxious worshippers. Temporary seats occupy the passages, and these are crowded, and many are content to stand at the door during the whole service. The very countenances of the worshippers declare the anxious and the happy feelings they possess, some seeming to say, ' Sir, we would see Jesus,' and others, ' we have tasted, and are now come to drink—we have found Him whom our souls love, and He is indeed precious." The thirst of the young for Sabbath-school instruction is intense and insatiable. Not less than fourteen hundred children attend every Sabbath morning, desiring the sincere milk of the Word, while my own class averages some eighty young men and women. We are reading the ' Confession of Faith,' and have circulated through the congregation some two hundred and fifty copies of it, with about an equal number of Paterson's Shorter Catechism. Social meetings for prayer, reading the Scriptures, and exhortation, are held throughout the parish, each district having its own prayer-meeting, and each prayer-meeting its own staff of conductors. No person is allowed to engage in the services unless approved of by these managers. The meetings are attended by the whole population, with very few exceptions—young and old, rich and poor, Episcopalian and Roman Catholic taking pleasure in listening to the simple prayers and earnest exhortations of their Presbyterian neighbours. The interest in them is still well sustained, and in the darkest, fiercest nights of winter, and now in the busiest days of seed-time, the number of those who meet together to thank and praise the Lord has not diminished.

" Previous to 1859 the voice of family prayer was seldom heard. Urgent appeals from the pulpit to erect a family altar were unheeded. Now family worship is rather the rule than the exception. There is a marked improvement in the public morals of the community. Men are ashamed of doings that formerly were considered things of course. Two public-houses have been obliged to close. The owners of others have assured me their trade is gone, and two more intimated their intention not to renew the licence. One of them said it was unsafe to himself and injurious to others. A deceased publican told him, he said, " that it was a cursed trade ; that he knew many in it, and, with two exceptions, he never knew one but the devil got a hold of, and these two had to give up and run, or he would have gotten them also.' Sabbath desecration, profane swearing, drunkenness, uncleanness, unseemly strife, and such like sins, are much abated and decreased, not one instance for every five we had in previous years ; while temperance, meekness, brotherly kindness, a holy reverence for the name and glory of God, have started into new life, and are putting forth new vigour. The Bible is the book of constant study. Many carry it about with them and read it by the wayside, or at intervals in their labour, and refer to it for the settlement of every disputed point. Two of our National School-houses have been enlarged, in order to make them capable of accommodating the prayer-meetings, and we have subscribed about £550 for a new church.

" It has been said that lay agency has done more harm than good in the successful promotion of revival work. My experience is the very reverse. I have seen indisputable proof that the Lord greatly honoured and blessed the zealous self-denying efforts of the Christian people. He touched their hearts, opened their mouths, and then rewarded their labours. Here they have been most useful auxiliaries to the ministry, and through their aid an amount of work has been overtaken which no half-dozen ministers could have performed. These young men deserve the highest praise, and I bear testimony that I have seen literally nothing of that overweening conceit and spiritual pride, so natural and so much feared by some good men.

Illustrative Cases.—" On the 12th of July the Orangemen of the district asked me to preach them a sermon ; about four thousand assembled in the open air without beat of drum or any insignia of their order, and after engaging in religious exercises, returned peaceably to their homes, no drink and no disorder appearing among them. On the Broughshane June fairday a band of strolling players as usual made their appearance ; a prayer-meeting was immediately convened opposite their showy platform. The players had but two visitors in the persons of two Roman Catholic policemen. The business of the fair was summed up by a prayer-meeting of not less than five thousand people.

" I saw a young girl in great distress about her soul, weeping bitterly ; her mother stood by and said, ' Oh, dear, why do you take on so ? ' The girl threw the shawl from her shoulders, dug her long bony fingers into the flesh of her naked bosom, and cried out, with bated breath, ' It's sin, sin, sin, cursed sin, here.' The mother, ' Oh, no, you were always a good girl.' ' Mother,' said the girl, ' don't talk that way to me ; I'm tempted sorely enough to think I'm not so bad, but oh, I am bad, very bad; oh, what a great sinner I am; Lord Jesus, have mercy on a poor, wicked, guilty wretch.' A young woman was forbidden by her employer—a minister of the Church of England—to go to the prayer-meeting, but if she was very anxious she might go down the back way and listen to what was said, through the wall of the churchyard where the meeting was held. That night she was awakened, and found peace. The next day the minister rebuked her, saying, 'How's this? did I not command you not to go there?' She replied, 'Yes, sir; but you said I might go down the back way, and God found me by the back way as well as if I had gone by the front way.'

"A lady remarked that she thought the presence of the Lord was very near to her; she almost felt as if God was in the air beside her. A man at the close of one of our prayer-meetings asked us to remember a poor stranger from Dungannon, who was in the midst of us, and anxious about his soul. Next night he came back and told us that he came to see the work of the Lord, and had found the Lord Himself; 'and this,' said he, 'was the way I found Him: I went up to my own little room, and took my Bible, and then went down on my knees and prayed over what I had read, and then read again, and then again prayed, and this is what I said in my prayer: 'Thou art a great God, and I am a poor sinner; I would come to Thee, but I have no offering to bring, no sacrifice to present, and Thou wilt not accept me without a sacrifice; O Lord Jesus, Thou hast a sacrifice; Thou hast offered Thyself a sacrifice; oh, present Thyself before the Father for me, and take me by the hand and lead me to Him, and make peace between us by the blood of Thy cross.' And then,' said he, ' I felt a movement in my soul, and the Saviour came and took me near, and I found there was peace between my Father and me; and now I am so happy.'

"A young man was passing along one day, and heard voices on the other side of the dyke. He looked and listened; three children were there, and one was in the exercise of prayer; when one finished another began; the third boy said he could not pray, and when urged, burst into tears; his two companions put his hands together, and said, 'Pray, mon; try it, if it be only the publican's prayer; say, God be merciful to me a sinner, and that will do.' The boy repeated the words, when one of the others said, 'There, now, may be that was the best prayer of the three.'

"A social tea-party met one night in a farmer's house. His wife, a very zealous Christian, felt that one of the guests had no right feelings about his precious soul. Something said to her she must not let this man away without faithfully warning him to seek the Lord. She retired to her closet and inquired of God what He would have her to do, but no plan was suggested to her. There was family worship; she felt the prayer was cold and not sufficiently pointed to warn her friend, about whom she was so suddenly interested. Just as they were all rising up from their knees, she could restrain her anxious feelings no longer, and, though contrary to her notions of female delicacy and duty, she burst forth in the most earnest and impassioned supplications, throwing out such warnings, and imploring such mercy for the careless, thoughtless ones of the number, as not only relieved her own breast of a burden, but sent a thrill to the heart of him for whom she felt so strongly.

"A poor man, after finding peace, said, 'Yesterday I was a poor, lone, desolate, friendless creature, caring for no one, and no one caring for me, without father or mother, house or friend; this day I am rich and happy, and would not exchange places with the Queen on the throne, for God is my Father, Christ Jesus is my Brother and Master, heaven is my home, and all God's people are my friends.'"

"It was towards the end of May 1859," says the Rev. H. W. Carson, "that the first symptoms of the great awakening began to discover themselves in the parishes of Lochguile, Kilraughts, and Dunaughy.

"The first in these parts deeply moved about her sins and eternal interests was a middle-aged woman. After six years' absence from the house of God, she felt a sudden inclination to return. The Word of God that Sabbath proved sharper than a two-edged sword. Her distress of mind grew deep; and never shall I forget the picture of misery she presented, as I found her sitting by the road-side wringing her hands, and, with upturned, tear-dimmed eyes, suing for mercy. Her sins were indeed many and dark, but she never saw them before in the same colours. Let us trust we can add, 'Her sins, which were many, have been forgiven her.' This woman may be regarded as the type of a large number who have passed 'through fire and through water into a wealthy place.'

"No doubt the Lord drew not a few gently under the shadow of His cross. There was a youth of fourteen who attended a monster prayer-meeting in the village of Cloughmills, when there could not have been less than 2000 present, and when the arrows of the King flew thick, so that many fell down before Him in penitence; and, as he afterwards related, he felt his heart opening to Christ, while tears flooded his eyes. Another, somewhat older, who has since often told the story of his conversion, and earnestly invited others to taste the grace that was so abundant to himself, acknowledged, 'Oh, He drew me in gentleness and love!' The hearts of these youths, and others like them, opened like the leaves of a rose to the light of morning. Sitting in the sanctuary ere the exercises commenced, a middle-aged man began to think of the blood of Christ, (to use his own description of his blessed experience,) thought he saw blood, and then his heart, in a stream, flowed towards Christ. He went quietly home, retired to thank God for the revelation of His Son in him, and soon began to experience joy unutterable. His exclamation, on first meeting me afterwards, was, 'Lovely! lovely!' 'What?' said I. He replied, 'Jesus is lovely.' This was indeed a revival, or a vivid revelation of Divine things. The man had spoken of Christ, thought of Christ, but never before had he such a clear and lively impression of Christ. He was ever to him an historical personage, but now He is a living reality with him, on the right hand and on the left.

"But while these were drawn gently, God dealt differently in the majority of conversions. Most passed through a terrible ordeal, and received, like Bunyan, a fiery baptism. Spectral-like, their sins affrighted them; mill-stonelike, their sins pressed them down. As the prisoner in the dock, hearing his sentence, and realising his awful death, has been known to shrink and swoon away, so, awakening to a sense of their condition, beholding the pit opening, and the devils come to drag them down, they have uttered doleful cries, heartrending shrieks. They have been carried out from the church; we have followed them to the green, and marked the writhings of the body, expressive of the commotion within; and we remember, while standing over the quivering frame of a youth, a convert, turning round to a stout man, a somewhat unmoved spectator of the scene, and saying, 'If sin does that in one so young, what must it do in the like of you, sir?'

"A noticeable stage in the spiritual history of the converts has been frequently that of severe mental struggle with infernal power. Satan, tenacious of his prey, has contended with the Saviour, and in the rage of disappointment and mortification of defeat, has thrown down, as in the days of Christ's sojourn on earth, the sinner coming; yea, has torn him in expulsion.

"Is liberality to missions a token of grace? There is a poor farmer who once gave only his sixpence on a day of missionary contribution, but now he lays down his pound-note, and feels it more blessed to give than to receive. It was thought this was done out of gratitude to God for reclaiming a vicious son. This may have been one reason, but the chief reason is that his own once-niggard heart has been enlarged—his once-closed hand has been opened by the Spirit of God. Are daily communings with the Host Migh significant of conversion? There are fifty houses which a heathen might have visited, and only discovered their inmates not to be heathens by the absence of everything like heathen devotion; lo, now they are 'the tabernacles of the righteous, in which is heard the voice of joy and rejoicing.' So strong is the testimony borne by the Spirit against the use of intoxicating drinks, that four public-houses in the parish have closed, and those publicans who remain in the trade find their occupation almost gone."

The Rev. Robert Park, for upwards of forty years the esteemed pastor of one of the Presbyterian churches in Ballymoney, writes as follows:—

"At nearly the close of a lengthened ministry to be permitted to see many of my charge brought to the Saviour, to know that some, over whom my heart has often yearned, are rejoicing in Jesus, and to believe that there are others in a hopeful state for eternity, has been not only gratifying, but greatly encouraging.

"As in other districts, the Divine sovereignty was exhibited here in the conversion of some of the despised of the people; but the larger proportion of those who have given evidence of a real saving change were con-

REVIVAL IN ITS PROGRESS NORTHWARDS

nected with our Sabbath-schools, either as teachers or receiving instruction, or were members of families well instructed in Divine truth, and more or less regular attendants on the means of grace. It was not the least interesting fact in the history of God's work here that He so touched the hearts of many young men who have since been zealously active in religious things.

"One most interesting case occurred in one of the country parts of my district. A man, about thirty years old, born *deaf and dumb*, who had been educated at the institution of Claremont, near Dublin, and who is in attendance on my ministry, was working in the bog, preparing fuel for the winter. He was alone, with no exciting appliance. The Lord touched his heart. He felt the pangs of sin and intense anxiety to have it removed. He endeavoured to make his way to his sister's house, where he resided. So prostrated was he in bodily strength, that he required to lie down and rest twice before he reached his home. During the night, and until the family were at breakfast the next morning, and preparing for public worship, it being the Sabbath, he was not relieved. The description of his manner and appearance, as given by his sister, was most striking. Literally, he jumped some height from the ground clasped as if some person to his bosom, his countenance beaming with delight, and his whole person indicating gratitude and love.

"In my conversation with him afterwards by fingers, he made me to understand that the first text of Scripture that impressed his mind and awakened comfort was Luke xv. 7, ' Joy shall be in heaven over one sinner that repenteth ; ' the second, 1 Tim. i. 15, ' This is a faithful saying, and worthy of all acceptation, that Christ Jesus came into the world to save sinners, of whom I am chief.' And again and again he laboured to shew me 'how happy he was in coming to Jesus.' In this, and in many instances that are before me, I fancy myself with Christ in the days of His ministry on earth, and almost see before my eyes the miracles that testified that He was the Messiah."

extra-biblical phenomena

6

The Revival in Northern Antrim

THERE is one incident so striking in the commencement of the movement in Coleraine, that it cannot be omitted in even the most cursory statement on the subject. It is impossible to present it in a better form than has been done by Mr Arthur, in one of his Tracts on the Revival. After narrating an impressive scene witnessed by one of his brethren, a Methodist minister in the town, he says:—

"Not far from the spot where this took place stands a large school, belonging to the corporation of London, or that body connected with it, known as the Irish Society, who are landlords of Coleraine and of much property around. In it a boy was observed under deep impressions. The master, seeing that the little fellow was not fit to work, advised him to go home, and call upon the Lord in private. With him he sent an older boy, who had found peace the day before. On their way they saw an empty house, and went in there to pray together. The two schoolfellows continued in prayer in the empty house till he who was weary and heavy-laden felt his soul blessed with sacred peace. Rejoicing in this new and strange blessedness, the little fellow said, 'I must go back and tell Mr ——.' The boy, who, a little while ago, had been too sorrowful to do his work, soon entered the school with a beaming face, and, going up to the master, said, in his simple way, 'O Mr ——, I am so happy; I have the Lord Jesus in my heart.' Strange words in cold times! Natural words, when upon the simple and the young the Spirit is poured out, and they feel what is meant by 'Christ in you the hope of glory,' and utter it in the first terms that come! The attention of the whole school was attracted. Boy after boy silently slipped out of the room. After a while, the master stood upon something which enabled him to look over the wall of the playground. There he saw a number of his boys ranged round the wall on their knees in earnest prayer, every one apart. The scene overcame him. Presently he turned to the pupil who had already been a comforter to one schoolfellow, and said, 'Do you think you can go and pray with these boys?' He went out, and, kneeling down among them, began to implore the Lord to forgive their sins, for the sake of Him who had borne them all upon the cross. Their silent grief soon broke into a bitter cry. As this reached the ears of the boys in the room, it seemed to pierce their hearts, as by one consent they cast themselves upon their knees, and began to cry for mercy. The girl's school was above, and the cry no sooner penetrated to their room than, apparently well knowing what mourning it was, and hearing in it a call to themselves, they, too, fell upon their knees and wept. Strange disorder for schoolmaster and mistress to have to control! The united cry reached the adjoining streets. Every ear, prepared by the Spirit, at once interpreted it as the voice of those who look upon Him whom they have pierced, and mourn for Him. One and another of the neighbours came in, and at once cast themselves upon their knees and joined in the cry for mercy. These increased, and continued to increase, till first one room, then another, then a public office on the premises, in fact, every available spot, was filled with sinners seeking God. Clergymen of different

The interdenominationalism of the revival: what would the Methodist minister have to say about the atonement? e.g. was it vicarious?

THE REVIVAL IN NORTHERN ANTRIM

denominations, and men of prayer, were sought, and they spent the day in pleading for the mourners;— sweetest of all the toils that earth can witness, when men, themselves enjoying heavenly peace, labour in intercession for those who are now, as they were once, broken-hearted by a sight of their sins, and striving to enter in at the strait gate, in order to walk in the narrow way! Thus passed hour after hour of that memorable day. Dinner was forgotten, tea was forgotten, and it was not till eleven o'clock at night that the school premises were freed from their unexpected guests."

The following statement respecting the movement in Coleraine is furnished by the Rev. J. A. Canning of that town :—

"Upon the evening of the 7th of June 1859, an open-air meeting was held in one of the market-places of the town, called the 'Fair-hill.' The announced object of the meeting was to receive and hear one or two of the 'converts,' as they began to be called, from a district some eight or ten miles south of Coleraine. The evening was one of the most lovely that ever shone. The richly-wooded banks of the river Bann, which bounds one side of the square in which the meeting was held, were fully in prospect, and there was not a cloud in the sky. Shortly after seven o'clock, dense masses of people, from town and country, began to pour into the square by all its approaches, and in a short time an enormous multitude crowded around the platform from which speakers were to address the meeting. After singing and prayer, the converts, a young man and a man more advanced in years, and both of the humbler class, proceeded to address the meeting. Their addresses were short, and consisted almost entirely of a detail of their own awakening, and earnest appeals to the consciences of sinners. After the lapse of nearly an hour, it became manifest that more than one-half of the congregated multitude could not hear the voices of the speakers on the platform, when it was suggested that the people should separate into distinct congregations or groups, and that a minister should preach to each group. This was immediately done, and some three or four separate audiences were soon listening with most marked attention to as many preachers, for all the ministers of all the evangelical churches in the town were present.

" I was engaged in addressing a large group of people, composed of all ages and of all ranks of the community, from a portion of Scripture, when I became struck with the deep and *peculiar* attention which manifestly every mind and heart was lending to what I spoke. As to manner, my address was very calm; and as to matter, it consisted of plain gospel truth, as it concerns man's lost condition on the one hand, and the free grace of God, as displayed in salvation, on the other, I know that the addresses of my brethren were of a like character. I never saw before, in any audience, the same searching, earnest, riveted look fixed upon my face as strained up to me from almost every eye in that hushed and apparently awe-struck multitude. I remember, even whilst I was speaking, asking myself, how is this? why is this? As yet, however, the people stood motionless, and perfectly silent; when, about the time at which the last speaker was closing his address, a very peculiar cry arose from out a dense group at one side of the square, and in less than ten minutes a similar cry was repeated in six or eight different groups, until, in a very short time, the whole multitude was divided into awe-struck assemblages around persons prostrate on the ground, or supported in the arms of relatives or friends. I hurried to the centre of one of these groups, and having first exhorted the persons standing around to retire, and leave me to deal with the prostrate one, I stooped over him, and found him to be a young man of some eighteen or twenty years, but personally unknown to me. He lay on the ground, his head supported on the knees of an elder of one of our churches. His eyes were closed; his hands were firmly clasped, and occasionally very forcibly pressed upon the chest. He was uttering incessantly a peculiar deep moan, sometimes terminating in a prolonged wailing cry. I felt his pulse, and could discern nothing very peculiar about it. I said softly and quietly in his ear, ' Why do you cry so ? ' when he opened his eyes for an instant, and I could perceive that they had, stronger than I ever saw it before, that inward look, if I might so express it, which indicates that the mind is wholly occupied with its own images and impressions. ' Oh ! ' he exclaimed, high and loud, in reply to my question, ' my sins ! my sins ! Lord Jesus, have mercy upon my poor soul ! O Jesus, come ! O Lord Jesus, come ! ' I endeavoured to calm him for a moment, asking him to listen to me whilst I set before him some of the promises of God to perishing sinners. At first I thought that I was carrying his attention with me in what I was saying, but I soon discovered that his whole soul was filled with one idea—his guilt and his danger ; for in the middle of my repetition of some promise, he would burst forth with the bitter cry, ' O God, my sins ! my sins ! ' At length I said in his ear, ' Will I pray ? ' He replied in a loud voice, ' Oh, yes ! ' I engaged in prayer, and yet I doubt whether his mind followed me beyond the first sentence or two. As I arose from prayer, six or eight persons, all at the same instant, pressed around me, crying, ' Oh, come and see (naming such a one)—and ——and ——'

until I felt for a moment bewildered, and the prayer went out from my own heart, ' God guide me ! ' I passed from case to case for two or three hours, as did my brethren in the ministry, until, when the night was far spent, and the stricken ones began to be removed to the shelter of roofs, I turned my face homewards through one street, when I soon discovered that the work which had begun in the market square was now advancing with marvellous rapidity in the homes of the people. As I approached door after door, persons were watching for me and other ministers, to bring us to deal with some poor agonised stricken one ; and when the morning dawned, and until the sun arose, I was wandering from street to street, and from house to house, on the most marvellous and solemn errand upon which I have ever been sent.

" Throughout the following day, the 8th of June, scenes similar to those which I have alluded to continued to occur in private houses in almost every street. In the evening a dense multitude assembled again in the market-place ; and again, simultaneously with the preaching of the gospel and prayer, many more than on the preceding evening sank upon the ground, and with bitter cries besought the Lord Jesus Christ to come in mercy to their souls. Profiting by the experience of the preceding night, elders of the churches and other Christian people sought now to find some building where the many 'stricken ones,' as they began now to be called, might receive shelter, and the attention of Christian ministers and others until the morning. Just at this period the new Town Hall of Coleraine had been completed, though it had never yet been used for any purpose. Some one suggested it as a fitting place of shelter. The suggestion was at once acted upon ; and a solemn interest attaches to the beautiful building from the fact that the first use for which it was ever employed was to shelter many, very many poor sinners, whilst they agonised with God for the pardon of sin.

"I may here mention that our Town Hall has been the scene, for seven months, of one of the most blessed fruits of God's gracious work among us. Early in June a meeting for united prayer, by members of all evangelical denominations, began to assemble at half-past nine o'clock, to continue for half-an-hour. For months the spacious hall continued to be filled at the appointed hour, and up to this day (January 12, 1860) a very large attendance of earnest worshippers assembles for praise and prayer. In the month of August the writer suggested that a copy of the Word of God should be purchased for the use of this union prayer-meeting, and to serve as a memorial to other times of the gracious work of God among us. The suggestion was very ardently adopted, and a copy of the Scriptures, of the largest size, and in very costly binding, was procured, and now, with a suitable inscription on the fly-leaf, appropriately and impressively witnesses every morning for Him who sent 'times of refreshing.'"

"As I wrote the last sentence, our local newspaper was put into my hands, and I extract from it the following statement from the bench of our local County Court, by a judge who would adorn any bench :—

"'The Barrister, addressing the Grand Jury, said—"When I look into the calendar for the last three months, and in memory look back on calendars that came before me, I am greatly struck with its appearance on this occasion. During the entire three months which have passed since I was here before, I find that but one new case has to come before you, and one which is in some respects very unimportant." After directing the jury as to this case, his Worship continued,—"Now, gentlemen, as I said before, I am greatly struck at the appearance of this calendar, so small is the number of cases, when I formerly had calendars filled with charges for different nefarious practices, pocket-picking, and larcenies of various sorts. Now, I have none of these, I am happy to say. How is such a gratifying state of things to be accounted for ? It must be from the improved state of the morality of the people. I believe I am fully warranted now to say that to nothing else than the moral and religious movement which commenced early last summer can the change be attributed. I can trace the state of your calendar to nothing else. It is a matter of great gratification when we see the people of this country improving, and I trust that no temptations of any sort will arise by which they can be induced to forsake the paths of rectitude." ' "

There is one incident, in the form of a personal narrative by an individual from Coleraine at a meeting in Glasgow, which is so extraordinary that it cannot be omitted here. I have made inquiry into the accuracy of the statements, and find them perfectly correct. The name of the narrator is Mr Haltridge :—

" It was in the year," he said, " when God was pouring out the vials of His wrath upon the three kingdoms, that I went to Coleraine. When the hand of God lay upon the place, many turned to the Lord ; but when it was removed, many turned like the sow that had been washed to her wallowing in the mire. He who stands before you was one of the latter sort. You see one before you who put out his wife to the door, and took her clothes, to the value of £20, and burned them. You see one before you who loaded his gun to shoot his own son. You see one before you who took a car and drove three miles to throw himself into the sea, and was found upon a rock with the billows dashing at his feet. And you would think that this was enough ; but not so. You see one before you who was tried for taking away the life of a fellow-creature. I tried to break the Sabbath-day in every possible manner. I took money in my pocket and went to Portrush and other watering-places to break the Lord's day. Not one in Coleraine would speak to me, and I did not give one in Coleraine the credit of being a Christian but one woman, who always spoke to me and asked for me when she saw me. On a Monday I went to my son, who was cashier, and took charge of my business, and demanded five pounds. It only lasted me that day. I demanded other five on Tuesday ; this lasted me till Saturday. The Rev. William Richey had overwrought himself with hard work, and was laid upon his bed. The doctor told him he had only half-an-hour to live (although he recovered after a lingering illness), and asked if he had any matters to arrange before he died. He pulled out a sealed packet from under his pillow, and said—' Will you give this to Mr Haltridge ? ' It was a few days after this the doctor gave me the package. (By this time I was brought under conviction.) He said he did not know what it was. I opened it. It was that little book, ' Come to Jesus.' I was in great distress one day, and I went away from my house about a quarter of a mile. I leaped over the wall and went into a summer-house there, in order that the dews of heaven might cool my fevered brow. I put my hand into my pocket to pull out my handkerchief, and that little book came into my hand. I would not give it for all Glasgow. One thing had escaped my memory. When the revival broke out, my son, a promising youth of twenty, although not brought under the grace of God, attended a meeting held at Market-Hill, and was ' stricken ' down. A good woman came to me while I was reading the flimsy trash of the day—'novels'—which I always did. She said—'Mr Haltridge, kneel down and give God thanks, your son is stricken down.' I ordered her to go out of the way, and went to my bedroom, and shut myself up for eight hours. They brought him and laid him on the sofa. I heard his cries. 'For twenty-four hours no one could tell whether he was dead or alive; but when God revealed himself to Him, the first thing he said was—' God be merciful to my wicked father.' I heard all this. My daughter attended meetings that were held in the school-house. She was 'stricken' down, and cried to God for mercy. The prayers of my Christian wife were now answered. She was a Christian from her youth up. I have seen her often at the bed side praying. I have taken the pillow and thrown it at her, at the same time lifting up my arm and defying God to do His worst. On Sabbath morning I was to go away to spend the Lord's-day in the same manner as before; but my wife came to the door and said, 'You will not go out to-day.' I drew back, and was for making my way out, but she and my daughter laid hold upon me, and drew me into the parlour, and reasoned with me until I promised to go to church. I went to the house of God. A hymn was given out to be sung. It was the same hymn that was blessed to the conversion of an actress. When I came to the second line, God laid His hand upon me; my book was trembling in my hands. My wife saw me going to fall, and let my head fall in her lap. I lay there for two hours. I was not sensible, but they told me I was crying for mercy. When I awoke I was surrounded by kind friends, who were praying for me; but the one that prayed loudest and longest was a boy, fourteen years of age, named John Hall. He had found the Lord himself, and he was crying, 'Lord reveal Thyself to Mr Haltridge.' My son took the

THE REVIVAL IN NORTHERN ANTRIM

one arm, and a kind friend the other, and helped me home. I was not able to walk; my feet refused to carry me. On reaching home I was laid upon that sofa on which, a month before, my son was laid. God opened my mouth that night to pray. I got peace from that text, ' Arise, and go thy way: thy sins, which are many, are forgiven thee; go and sin no more.' I now felt such love to my fellow-men that I thought I could stand on a mountain top and take the whole world in my arms. And as Christ told His disciples to begin preaching at Jerusalem, I was called upon to speak at meetings held in that place which has been the scene of my former life."

Nowhere, perhaps, was there a more interesting movement than in Portrush, one of the principal wateringplaces in the north, a few miles from the Giant's Causeway and during the whole season crowded with visitors, many of whom, there is reason to believe, were sharers in the blessing. I have received a lengthened narrative from the Rev. Jonathan Simpson, from which I give the following selections:—

" By a strange coincidence in Divine providence, both the clergy of the parish church and the Presbyterian minister of Portrush were attracted to Ballymoney in the same week, without any previous concert with each other, to see and investigate the remarkable work of revival going on there in its earliest stages. The former called on the latter, and proposed an open-air unionmeeting for prayer, into which he cordially entered; and the three knelt in prayer in the manse, craving a blessing on the proposed meeting, led by the senior Episcopal minister. Their hearts were melted by the love of Christ, and they felt that God was about to give a blessing; nor were they disappointed; blessed be His name!

"The meeting took place on the 6th of June, on the hill in the rear of the town, and was very large, probably two thousand being present : the town contains a population of about nine hundred souls. Short addresses of only a few minutes were delivered by the local ministers and several persons, usually called 'converts' from Ballymoney ; and a very remarkable scene took place, that will never be forgotten in the village, or by many of its inhabitants in eternity. The first two 'stricken' ones were, one a Presbyterian, and the other an Episcopalian, as if God would honour the first union prayer-meeting.

"Next morning assembled the first daily union prayer-meeting, which was continued with great success till the close of the bathing season in September. As many as one hundred and fifty-one have been counted leaving it, and in some instances several went away who could not get in ; while a ball-room, erected during the summer, could get none to dance in it. The first two mornings a young man, in each case, came under conviction of sin— one Episcopal, the other a Presbyterian.

"The churches were crowded all summer. The Episcopal church has been enlarged, and the Presbyterian would require to be double its present capacity, to contain the anxious applicants for accommodation.

"Brownlow North, Esq., visited most opportunely, and, by his earnest and thrilling appeals largely contributed to advance the glorious cause. He preached twice in the Presbyterian church, Portrush, and addressed two open-air meetings, one in the town and the other at Dunmull. The latter was the noblest meeting ever seen in the neighbourhood ; the very sight was grand, apart from its bearings on eternity. Mr North, accustomed to large audiences, computed it at sèven thousand ; and so many were stricken that day, that the people in the neigh-

THE REVIVAL IN NORTHERN ANTRIM

bouring houses never got to bed the entire night, so many hearts were bleeding under a sense of sin, and weeping over a pierced Saviour."

From the numerous cases furnished by Mr Simpson, I select the following as representative of many others:—

An Operation of the Spirit.—" On Tuesday morning, 7th June, before going out to the prayer-meeting at seven o'clock, a farmer called at the manse wanting to speak privately to the minister. 'What have you to say to me?' 'Sir, *I have got an operation of the Spirit.*' Wonderful spiritual surgery that, that cuts out ' the hard and stony heart out of the flesh,' and substitutes ' a heart of flesh!' Such ' an operation ' H. C—— had got. He had gone home from the union open-air prayer-meeting deeply impressed; the burden of sin lay so heavy on his soul he could not sleep. He rose from his partner's side without telling her of the tempest of agony sweeping his bosom, dressed, took the key of his barn, went there to fall upon his knees, and, like Jacob, ' wrestle with the Angel Jehovah-Jesus till the dawn of the day,' and say, ' I will not let thee go, except thou bless me.' Like the patriarch he wrestled, like him he sped. He got ' an operation of the Spirit,' and, without waiting till his wife was up, he came away to tell the minister, and to ask him if he should make known to others the work of grace on his soul.

The Railway Labourer.—" Next evening, after returning from country visits, a man was sitting for me at the manse. He is a railway labourer, had been at the Monday evening meeting, been deeply impressed, and under sore exercises of a sense of sin ever since—had often, during the week, left the other men on the line, and gone behind the fence to weep. At last the proud heart, brought down by conquering grace, must seek relief in counsel, and he came down on a freight-truck attached to a train, and literally ran from the station to seek the minister. On reaching the school, and finding from my teacher I was not at home, the pent-up feelings found relief to a flood of tears. The teacher, a worthy, excellent young man, offered all the counsel he could—came with J. M—— to the manse, and prayed with him—took him to one of the elders, who also offered counsel and prayer—and sent for the curate, who kindly came and spoke and prayed with him. Still he remained ; and when I entered told his story of guilt, while he sat trembling and said he had broken every commandment of God except the sixth and eighth. Besides that, he never set foot in a place of worship, nor bowed the knee to God. On one occasion he was so drunk he lay down on the rails, and only for some one passing and hauling him off, he had been, by the next train, a mangled corpse, and his poor soul in hell ; and then he asked if it was possible such a sinner could get mercy. ' Perfectly so, for God says it—" The blood of Jesus Christ his Son cleanseth us from all sin." " Him that cometh unto me, I will in no wise cast out." ' (1 John i. 7 ; John vi. 37.) After a few more words of counsel, prayer was offered, and he withdrew greatly relieved. He was a young married man, father of ten children, and had no connection with any place of worship. Since then he has been most regular, has also established the worship of God in his family, and has a weekly prayer-meeting in his house. His wife and eldest daughter were both afterwards ' stricken,' and the three were among nine pleaders before my session to dispense with the usual lengthened examination for the Lord's Supper, and admit them at our last communion. They were admitted, and ' go on their way rejoicing.'

The Ploughboy.—" During the prayer in a farm-house

one day, there was much emotion. At its close, a tall, stout, able-bodied young man, twenty years of age, R. R——, the farmer's eldest son, approached one of the ministers trembling, and seizing him by the hand as tears flowed fast—'Mr S——, you can't leave.' 'Why, Robert?' 'Oh, you can't leave me in this state!' 'Why what's wrong?' 'Oh, I'm so ill—*such a load upon my heart!*' 'But can't you go with your load to the cross, and Jesus will take it from you? He says, "Come unto me, *all ye that labour and are heavy laden*, and I will give you rest."' 'Oh, but I can't go.' 'Can't you pray Christ to take you?' 'No, I'm so ill, I can't; will you pray?' So saying, he fell on his knees before me, and I had to proceed in prayer. He had just come in from the plough, with his horses, in time to catch the prayer that, by the Spirit's grace, enabled him to 'put his hand to *another* plough,' and I thank God he has *not* 'looked back.'

The Old Waterloo Man.—"An old soldier of the Duke of Wellington, whose regiment had been disbanded after Waterloo, now seventy-three years of age, had stood, till late in the evening, watching a poor Roman Catholic girl whom some Christian ladies had removed to their house. Next morning early, the old soldier's wife was down for the minister. Having so many visits to make that day, even with a good steed, it was afternoon before I reached the old man. He sat up in bed half-dressed, and was in an awful agony of prayer, hands clasped, tears pouring, without any attempt to wipe them away. His attention was diverted for a few seconds by my presence, and after tightly grasping my hands for a minute he burst out again in a tempest of prayer, of which this is a specimen:—"O blessed Saviour of the world, melt this hard heart, this wretched heart! It is a hard heart, a wretched heart. O blessed Saviour, pour out Thy Holy Spirit on every wretched sinner like me! Oh, a heart pressed down!' 'Pressed down with what, Billy?' I interposed. He replied, 'Sin—Satan!' and then proceeded in prayer:—' O Saviour, free me! Oh, wash me in "the fountain opened!" Oh, plunge me in it! I know He'll not "put my soul to shame, nor let my hope be lost." O blessed Saviour, I won't distrust you one jot! O dear Saviour, dear Lord and Saviour, forsake me not!' When asked what enabled him to pour out such prayers, he replied, 'It is nothing but the work of heavenly love by the Holy Spirit;' and catching the idea of 'heavenly love,' he interwove it in prayer:—' O Heavenly Love, subdue me! Oh, He will be my Friend!' When I asked what I should pray for when I knelt beside him, he replied, 'For the abundant outpouring of the Holy Spirit on this wretched heart, and on all that desire Him.' Be it remembered the old man can't read a word.

The Twin Sisters.—" The following is a case of sisters who were affected at the Dunmull meeting:—They continued to pray night and day, 'Lord, remember me '—so much so, that their mother has informed me she has heard them repeating it through their sleep. A faithful God listened to artless country girls of sixteen years of age, the only surviving children of their parents, and at the close of a prayer-meeting in the neighbourhood both were 'remembered.' And how precious the thought that the God of love gave both the second birth the same night, as He had done the natural birth! On our first visit after the 'Lord remembered them,' the fountains of feeling were unsealed, and gave forth their sparkling treasures. It was moving to see the girls sitting side by side repeating alternate verses of the 12th chapter of Isaiah. An old gentleman from London, and a rector of Hereford, England, accompanied me. The latter asked to be allowed the privilege of praying in that house, and remarked when we passed out, ' I wish my bishop had been here to-day. I think he would have altered his next charge to his clergy about the Irish revival ; ' and the old Londoner, who was very much overcome, when he had dried his cheeks, lifted up both hands, and exclaimed, ' Well, if this be hysteria, God grant that London may be soon smitten with it ! '

"From a journal kept from time to time, these details are merely excerpts. My record covers over three hundred cases, I dare not say of conversion, but I must say of the mighty Spirit's power to ' convince the world of sin.' From contact with this ' wonderful work of God,' and being honoured to take some little part in carrying it on, my spirit has been literally overwhelmed with a sense of my own deep unworthiness ; but it were worth living ten thousand ages in obscurity and reproach to be permitted to creep forth at the expiration of that time, and engage in the glorious work of the last six months of 1859."

7

The Revival in the Capital of Ulster

TRAVELLING from Scotland in the end of May, in company with the Rev. J. H. Moore, of Connor, after the meeting of the Free Church Assembly, the conversation between us naturally turned upon the extraordinary movement then in progress in our native land. Intelligence received from home during the ten days previously had informed us of its rapid spread over the country; and it was further announced that some of the young men from Connor were about to visit the metropolis of the north, there to make known the great things they had witnessed in connection with the work of God. I ventured to express a somewhat unfavourable opinion of the proposed mission, when my fellow-traveller said, " I have so often seen how human wisdom has been at fault in this whole movement, that I should not wonder if the employment of such an agency as that in question should be extensively blessed for good, and if the visit of our friends should be only preparatory to a great awakening among your fellow-townsmen."

Two days after it was matter of record in the local journals that the revival tide had " set in " in Belfast. On the Sabbath evening previous a very solemn meeting had been held in Linenhall Street Church, when the strangers referred to described the remarkable work going on in their own neighbourhood, and impressed all present by their simple and touching statements. Near the close

Unauthorised addresses.

[handwritten at top: illegitimate/disorderly speaking leading to "a commotion". Contrary to the scripture: "let all things be done in order"]

of the service, a female, who, it was said, had gone incredulous as to the reality of the movement, was affected in a manner similar to what had been witnessed in other places; while others who had attended, both male and female, were reported as being seized with religious convictions in their own dwellings.

On the evening of Tuesday a meeting was held in another church, when, after addresses by the visitors from Connor, a strange commotion took place in the audience. A young woman first, then a young man, cried for mercy. After the usual dismissal the people lingered behind in hundreds, partly in amazement at what had taken place before their eyes, and partly for an additional opportunity of engaging in exercises of devotion. The building was reopened, and the pastor, the Rev. Hugh Hanna, who had been engaged up to this period elsewhere, presided. Next morning groups of interested persons were congregated around the dwellings of those who had been "affected" on the preceding evening. The general impression was that the great realities which had been witnessed elsewhere had come amongst us, and that the gracious rain which had so copiously fallen in other places was about to descend in plenteous effusion throughout our borders.

A week later the whole community was agitated by the unusual visitation. In the churches on the Sabbath attention had been directed by the respective pastors to the all-engrossing theme, while a feeling of deepest solemnity pervaded the congregations. In the course of a few days religious meetings were commenced in many districts of the town, some of which had not long before acquired an unhappy notoriety as the scenes of party animosity and even bloodshed. Every available agency was put into requisition to meet the exigency;

and it became necessary for ministers to beg the co-operation of teachers in Sabbath-schools, and other friends, in attending to the awakened, as they themselves were even already almost worn out with work.

At an early period in the history of the revival in Belfast the ecclesiastical authorities, as might have been expected, took an opportunity of declaring their judgment with regard to it. The Bishop of the Diocese, at all times ready to identify himself with every enterprise bearing upon the moral elevation of the community, took part in a series of discourses in course of delivery on the subject by one of his clergy, and expressed the most generous sentiments with respect to all, of whatever denomination, who were engaged in the advancement of this great work.

The Rev. Dr Miller, vicar, inserted a letter in the papers in which he said—" Whatever be the issue of this movement, one thing, at least, is *now* evident, that amongst the people generally there is an awakening from spiritual death, an anxiety after the soul's salvation, and a growing desire for the means of grace. All this is a subject of deep gratitude and thankfulness to the Author and Giver of all good things."

The ministers of the Wesleyan and Independent bodies threw themselves into the movement with characteristic energy; as also did the Presbytery of Belfast.

A week later a united meeting for prayer—the first of a series which was long continued weekly—was held in the Music Hall, the Mayor in the chair. The building being crowded to excess, while nearly a hundred ministers of all denominations filled the platform. That which was held on the following week was presided over by the Bishop of Down and Connor, and was so numerously attended that hundreds who were unable to gain admittance engaged in similar exercises in another part of the building.

Toward the end of the month, it having been considered desirable by some to bring together in one place the friends of the movement in the surrounding districts, the grounds of the Botanic Gardens were thrown open for the purpose, and an assemblage convened such as was never seen before in the north of Ireland. I was not of those who looked with special favour on the proposal to collect together a miscellaneous multitude whom it might be difficult to control, and over whom no human voice by possibility could reach; while the idea of such a gathering seemed rather to suggest that of a " demonstration " of mere numbers than of a holy convocation assembled for Divine worship. Nor, after the experience of two such meetings in which I have borne a part, have I seen cause to form a different judgment respecting them. At the same time, I must declare that there was that in the settled demeanour and orderly array of those unprecedented assemblies, which presented to the beholder the finest specimen of true moral sublimity. A friend came to me as I was about to join the moving mass that thronged our streets on their way thither, one as calmly philosophic as he is earnestly Christian in all his aims, and said, " Well, I have been looking on for the last half-hour on the most impressive spectacle I ever witnessed. I have seen in my own country, when a youth, some mighty gatherings, especially during the agitation for Reform, and have stood by when thousands of sturdy and resolute men were congregated, whose very tramp had a stern purpose in it; but I have never been so impressed by any such exhibition as by the calm and earnest look of those plain men and women, with their Bibles in their hands, who are pouring on in an unceasing stream toward the Gardens. I have not, as you know, been satisfied as to the wisdom of the course that has brought all these people here, but I feel that I must join them in their solemn exercises. Come, then, and let us go."

Commanding the open space in which they met, the towers of the Queen's College peering through the trees, and the Cavehill in rugged majesty bounding the further view, stood the covered platform, or rather pavilion, which on that occasion served as the pulpit for the officiating brethren. From the same position the most extraordinary of living preachers, the Rev. Mr Spurgeon, had about a year before proclaimed the message of mercy to listening thousands. But now the occasion was not one of preaching, but of prayer. These waiting multitudes had come together not to hang upon the eloquence of man, but to fall down prostrate before the throne of God. From the crowded lanes and alleys of our town—from the lone hamlets of the hills and cabins of the villages, all round for thirty or forty miles, they had come forth that day—many of them with hearts enlarged and full of new-born love—having bent the knee before they left their homes, and fervently implored a blessing on the devotions which they had sought to share. As they arrived from one and another region round about, the citizens stood amazed at their accumulating numbers, many an onlooker being led to inquire within himself whereunto this would grow. The great majority were strangers, who, as they passed through the crowded thoroughfares, took no heed of any of their attractions. Nothing of holiday *abandon* was seen upon them—nothing of the promptings of mere curiosity, or admiration of the summer glories of the scene, diverted them from the grand object for which they had assembled. And now the thirty or forty thousand—for they were differently estimated—had met under the open canopy of heaven, and there with one accord were sending up their common supplications to the mercy-seat, or filling all the air with their melodious praise.

It is not necessary to describe in detail the proceedings of that solemn meeting. The presidential chair was filled by the then Moderator of the General Assembly, the apostle and patriarch of open-air assemblies for public worship. During the exercises were heard many cries for mercy; and although the proceedings lasted for four hours, order reigned so far as was possible among such a multitude. Here and there, however, were distinct groups of worshippers—some led by those of tender years, others addressed by ministers or laymen. In the outskirts there were occasionally some questionable scenes, but the peculiar character of the exercises rendered it impossible for any one to interpose by rational expostulation. Such extravagances, however, were comparatively rare, and there is no doubt that many subsequently traced their first impressions to that day. By five o'clock the town was completely cleared of its unwonted visitors, and in a few hours afterwards those who had come from a distance were again in their respective homes.

On the way homewards, the engagements of many partook of the spirit of the services of the forenoon. Some friends who had been at Portrush were returning to town that evening; and as they met the excursion train with its freight of seven hundred passengers at Antrim, their ears were saluted by a loud outburst of melody from the occupants of the third-class carriages, as with one voice and soul they sang together the well-known revival lyric, " What's the News ? "

Of those who date their saving change from the Great Garden meeting, the following is a pleasing specimen :—

In the course of the proceedings, a strong and powerful man, who went from mere curiosity, was attracted to one of the side groups where a youthful individual was addressing those around him. At a certain point in the service a request was made that all should kneel down in prayer, as an act of submission to the Lord Jesus Christ. Slowly and reluctantly our visitor complied. He rose under great mental depression, and left the ground under an agonising sense of sin. He returned to his home in town, and subsequently, in hope of finding some relief, he started for his mother's house, some seven miles distant; but no peace for him was *there*. He sought the prayer-meeting, but left it as he came, his burden still unremoved. That night upon his bed he had a sustaining view of Christ, beheld by faith. Next morning, finding a Christian friend who was at his daily occupation in the field, he asked an interest in his prayers. They knelt together, and had not long been in that posture till he sank into an unconscious condition, and so remained for upwards of two hours. When he arose the burden had fallen off, and he felt light and joyful in the Lord. Returning home another man, his first resolve was to give up the spirit trade in which he had been engaged, a resolution which he at once carried into effect. In the full joy of his heart he stood up unsolicited in the face of a meeting assembled for prayer one evening, and avowed his change, taking as the ground of his remarks, " Therefore being justified by faith, we have peace with God through our Lord Jesus Christ." And ever since he has been enabled to witness a good confession; while God has blessed his conversion and example, his prayers and labours, as a means of bringing other strong men like himself to the feet of Jesus.

A week or two previously, having been requested by

the Rev. Hugh Hanna—to whose congregation a signal blessing has been vouchsafed—to aid him in one of his evening meetings, it devolved on me, after the introductory devotional services, to deliver a short address to those assembled, by whom the church was densely filled—as, indeed, it was on successive evenings for months together. Anxious to repress any tendency to mere excitement, I endeavoured to set forth in the most didactic and unimpassioned strain the way of salvation, avoiding every allusion that might be calculated to awaken mere emotion in any of the audience. I had not, however, proceeded far, until there arose from a female voice a despairing and yet tender cry, accompanied by a sinking of the bodily energies, insomuch that she had to be borne from the place of meeting. This case was soon after succeeded by another and another, until it became necessary to suspend the address in course of delivery, and engage in singing, until all who were affected had been removed. After this the service proceeded without further interruption to its close, if close it could be called, as after the benediction the congregation kept their seats, and showed no disposition to retire. It was necessary, therefore, to resume, and again address the thirsting multitude. The benediction was a second time pronounced, and yet they lingered in the sanctuary. At length the place was cleared, and I accompanied the minister and one or two other brethren to the library, to which the affected parties had been removed. That apartment being densely filled by themselves and their attendant relatives and friends, they were immediately taken into the adjoining gallery of the church. There they remained, some for a shorter, others for a longer period, until they were sufficiently recovered to be conveyed home. All were apparently labouring under the pressure of an intolerable burden. One, about fourteen years of age, had begun to emerge out of "the depths" of her soul-sorrow, and was speaking very touchingly of the grace and beauty of the Saviour. In the case of the majority (I think there were from twelve to fifteen—all females,) human help was manifestly unavailing, and we could only commit them to the tenderness of the Divine compassion. There was one of the cases which I had no doubt was hysterical, and nothing more. The young woman was violently vociferous and convulsive; whereas in the others there was nothing of convulsive movement whatsoever.

The next day, having taken down their addresses, I visited at their own houses some of the "stricken" of the preceding evening. In the first house I entered I found the girl in bed, conscious and intelligent, but not yet recovered out of the first stage of her prostration. By her side sat a sister, who had herself been similarly affected, but who had found relief from her mental anguish, although she seemed to have but a scanty knowledge of the gospel. Seated in the kitchen, however, I observed, on entering, a young female, in whom I became at once deeply interested. She was tidily but plainly dressed, and on her countenance was an expression of "perfect peace"—it was, indeed, lit up with a look of radiant joy. She had a Bible in her hand; and in answer to my questions she stated that a short time previously she herself had undergone in the same church a similar process to that which was now so common, and was rejoicing in God her Saviour. She was employed in a weaving factory in town, and "as her web was out," and she had a day to herself, she had taken the opportunity of making the rounds of some of her acquaintances, who had been the subjects of a like spiritual transition. She had been a Sabbath-school scholar, and showed a thorough acquaintance with her Bible. She spoke of her " good hope through grace " with unshaken confidence, though sensible at the same time that clouds and darkness might now and then assail her in the Christian pilgrimage. She cared for little now—for nothing, indeed, of the earth. Even her daily food was scarcely necessary to her. " Christ was her meat and drink," and she was happy in him.

Being in attendance some weeks after at one of the mid-day meetings of the mill-girls held in the school-house in connection with Linenhall Street Church, I was witness to a touching scene. One of the females present, towards the close of the exercise, was seized with an extreme weakness. She did not raise a cry, nor did she use any words, but her downcast look and tearful countenance told of the conflict that was going on within. Several ministers were present, one of whom, an Episcopal rector from a distance, offered up an impressive prayer. By and by, when others had fallen off from her who had excited so much solicitude, one of her fellow-workers, who was in the little meeting, was seen hasting to her side, and kneeling down amid the hushed attention of all present, was heard to offer up a fervent and most appropriate supplication for the afflicted one. It was a truly affecting scene. The offerer of the consolation I recognised at once as my young friend, whom I had met before on her errand of sympathy with the sisters of the family whom I had first visited. I asked her at the close how matters went with her now, when she at once replied that she was quite happy in Christ, and had " got more love." I have seen her once and again since, and have reason to believe that she continues steadfast and exemplary, and has in her humble way proved " a succourer of many."

But to resume. Calling at another house adjacent, I found a young woman seated in the apartment, perfectly calm and collected, but in a condition of deep and despairing agony. Sitting by her side was one of her own sex, upon whose countenance was a very different aspect, the unmistakable indication of a reigning serenity within. In the course of our conversation, I learned in a few words her spiritual history. She had, according to her statement, been brought up a member of a pious family, but had not until a short time before known in her own experience anything of the power of piety. On the contrary, she had no concern about the one thing needful, and put away all tendency to serious thought. When the revival came, and others were attending meetings every evening, she resolved that she would resist every solicitation to be present at them, caring for none of these things. One day, however, when at her work (she was engaged in a sewed muslin establishment in town), she was arrested all at once by a sight of her own sinfulness, and laid her head upon the bench before her, that she might give herself up to solemn meditation. No sooner had she done so than, under the prompting of an uncontrollable impulse, she fell down on her knees and cried imploringly for mercy. Others of her fellow-workers were looking on, and in the midst of her distress it came into her mind, at the suggestion, she believed, of Satan, that she was subjecting herself to the imputation of great weakness by such a public exhibition of her private griefs, but, rebuking the insinuation of the deceiver, she cried all the more earnestly, and ere long had such a view of Christ, and such a sense of His wondrous love, that when she arose she could rejoice in the assurance of a present salvation. And now, she also was making a few calls on those of whom she had heard as being sought out of the same loving Saviour who had come to her in such a time as she desired Him not. As our interview proceeded, a young woman entered the place, the same, I at once observed, whose case I had regarded as mere hysteria the previous evening, and whose demeanour did not now furnish any satisfactory evidence to the contrary. On being asked whether she had any evidence of her acceptance in the sight of God, she answered that the weight was still about her heart, and that for relief she was about to return to the prayer-meeting in the evening. My fellow-visitor, whose case I have narrated, said to me, when subsequently referring to the experience of this other, that she regarded it as far from hopeful, as the young woman in question seemed to be going after meetings, instead of going at once to Christ.

I paid a third visit in another part of the town, to a house in which one of the inmates, a young girl, was laid upon the bed, also in the first stage of physical prostration. The old man, her father, who received me, said he was not sorry, indeed, to see her there. She had been borne in in that state from the meeting the previous night, and he hoped that, when she recovered, she would be different from what she ever had been before. Her temper was in great need of improvement; and if the same result took place with her as with her sister, who had been affected as she was, it would be a blessed change for her and them. The next time I called, he assured me that his expectations had been fully realised respecting his daughter. "And now," said he, "there's not a better girl in all the neighbourbood."

In company with my old friend, the father, who said

that he knew at least forty in that district who were brought under the same gracious influence, I called on a young man who had a short time before, as was represented, experienced a wondrous change: He had been a "good-for-nothing fellow," spending his earnings in the public-house, frequenting no place of worship, lounging about the fields upon the Sabbath, a fearful swearer, and a dog-fighter. We visited the miserable hovel, scarcely eight feet square, which served as the abode of himself, his wife, and three little children, and found that he had not recovered sufficient strength to enable him to return to his work on the railway hard by, but that he was calling on some others in the vicinity who had been brought to themselves as he was. We heard from his wife, before he returned, his striking story. She had herself, she said, been brought to Christ at one of the meetings ; and though he was very averse to go, she had prevailed on him about a fortnight before to accompany her to Linenhall Street Church, where an address was being delivered by some Scottish minister. She prayed inwardly that the word might reach her husband's heart. Scarcely had she sought for mercy on his behalf, when, looking round to observe his looks, she saw him all at once turn deadly pale, and then, with a loud cry, he fell to the earth, and had to be removed from the place of meeting. He was in great agony of mind afterwards, but had found peace ; and now what a change! What sometimes affected him was his straitened circumstances, and his inability, not yet having regained his strength, to go about his work. The other day, looking at her and the children in want of bread, he had burst out into a fit of crying; but she had cheered him up, and, handing him the Bible, bid him read a chapter, for she could not read herself ; which done, he offered up a prayer, and then was as happy as ever. By this time the husband had returned, when he confirmed all we had heard respecting him. "I was indeed," said he, "a drunken rascal—nothing less; and all my pleasure was to drink and sin. But, blessed be His name, I have seen a sight which has made me another man." And then he went on to narrate, in simple yet eloquent language, the mode in which the spiritual transition had been realised. He was lying on his bed writhing under the burden of sins; and such a burden! He saw his sins rolling down like mountains of lead upon him, and he felt that they must sink him to perdition. But presently he saw ("that is," he continued, "I *thought* I saw") a glorious Being rising up before him with sweet countenance, and bearing on Him the marks of being crucified; and as He drew near, the mountains of sin began to sink down out of view, until at last they were all gone, and nothing was to be seen but a loving Saviour. "I think," he said, "I see Him still, and I wish, if it be His will, never to let Him out of my sight." And then he went on to say how he loathed the practices he had loved. Whisky was now his abomination, and he would not for the world enter the place where it was sold; and as for profane swearing, he did not feel the least temptation to it; and when at any time he saw that an oath was coming out of the lips of any one, it made his very bones tremble. I have once and again visited this interesting couple in humble life, and I have every reason to believe that they continue to walk together in love, and that theirs is, in the highest sense of the word, a happy home. They have, some months ago, quitted their former wretched habitation, and are now enjoying the substantial comforts of a commodious dwelling.

Not to dwell, however, on individual instances, I shall

here introduce an interesting communication respecting the work in another district in the outskirts of the town. The place is called Ewart's Row, and is inhabited altogether by mill-workers. The proprietors of the mill, the principal of whom is our present excellent chief magistrate, lent every facility to their work-people to avail themselves of the opportunities of religious instruction which were so abundantly enjoyed, and have had their reward in the improved habits of their little community. The writer of the subjoined statement is a young female, the daughter of a respectable tradesman, whose own spiritual history is deeply interesting. Up to the 29th of June she was altogether frivolous in her tastes, and fond of gaiety and worldly amusements. She had, however, been importuned by a friend to attend a meeting in the Rev. Hugh Hanna's church, on the evening of the day in question, and very reluctantly complied. In the course of the service, a young woman fell down by her side, and in the act of rising to follow and render her assistance, she herself was similarly seized. Having been removed to her own home, she was for several days subjected to extreme bodily weakness, her mind being all the while in " perfect peace." On her recovery under the prompting of an earnest desire to do good to others, she opened a class for the instruction of her sisters in the " Row," so many of whom had been themselves the subjects of the merciful visitation. Although in the subjoined statement she makes no reference to herself, it is well known that the enterprise owes its success largely to her devoted labours :—

" Ewart's Row is a manufacturing suburb of Belfast, on the north side of the town, having a population of about fifteen hundred souls. It was visited by the grace of God at an early period of the revival. Many were brought to a saving knowledge of Jesus in a very remarkable way. The change that was thus manifested, and the earnest entreaties and fervent prayers of the converts for the salvation of their friends and neighbours, by the Divine blessing, awakened the whole locality. There was no district of Belfast so deeply moved. The whole population crowded to prayer-meetings and open-air preachings, evincing the deepest seriousness and concern about eternal things. Every one betook himself to the prayerful reading of the Bible. Those who could read but imperfectly or not at all, bewailed their inability; every one became eager for instruction in the Word of God. At this crisis the Ewart's Row school was opened by the district-visitors connected with the Berry Street church. Christian friends from other congregations joined in the good work, and the Lord has crowned their labour with abundant success. The average attendance on three evenings during the week is about one hundred and fifty. Many of the girls who could read but very imperfectly at the opening of the school, in three months had committed the whole of the Shorter Catechism; others, the greater portion of the Book of Psalms; and many, portions of the Scriptures. Their memories are stored with the Word of God. Their hearts fondly cherish it, and their lives are beautifully regulated by its requirements. Useful branches of instruction have been introduced. Many of the poor girls now write a beautiful hand. Some have advanced considerably in arithmetic. Industrial occupations have engaged the time of others, who will shortly be better fitted for domestic duties.

"The good done in every direction is incalculable. Scripture classes and prayer-meetings are without end in the district. The excitement attendant on the earlier stages of the revival has passed away, but a deep and settled seriousness remains, the result, it is believed, of the saving grace of God. The greatest happiness that earth can afford is enjoyed by teachers and scholars in their schools and prayer-meetings. The teachers delight in the work, and confess that the hours spent in Ewart's Row have been among the happiest of their lives. The Lord has done great things for us. The change witnessed in the locality is astonishing. The leisure hours were formerly devoted to boisterous amusements, in which profane swearing was practised to a fearful extent; now the name of God is never heard but with reverence on any lips. Both sexes have shared in the grace of God, and Ewart's Row is now a regenerated locality."

Among those who visited us at this time none were more highly prized, either in Belfast or elsewhere, than Mr Brownlow North, to whom reference has been made in connection with the great meetings at Portrush. The striking spiritual history of Mr North himself, his social status, and the wonderful success attending his labours, especially for the preceding two years in Scotland, all contributed to concentrate public attention on his evangelistic labours. He came to Belfast in the end of June, and did not leave Ulster for two months afterwards. During the intermediate period he was employed incessantly in public ministrations, and had abundant evidence that his labour was not in vain. Rooms were put at his service by a devoted lady in Donegall Place, in which he was daily consulted by many members of the wealthier class.

Having had frequent opportunities of hearing this eminent servant of Christ during his sojourn here, I can bear testimony to the wonderful power of his addresses —for sermons, in the usual acceptation of the term, they

REVIVAL IN THE CAPITAL OF ULSTER

cannot be designated; although, however, there was no attempt at methodical arrangement or rhetorical art, yet such was the intense and outbreaking energy of the speaker, that every one felt compelled to listen. Thousands and thousands were gathered around him; and whether under the canopy of heaven, or in the largest buildings that could be thrown open to receive him, he was ever ready to proclaim that truth which in his own case he had found inestimably precious. His visits to the awakened districts were peculiarly seasonable. In many cases, those who regarded themselves as brought under saving influence were disposed mainly to rest for comfort on their own experience of pardon and of the preciousness of Christ. With reiterated fulness of demonstration he exposed the futility of relying on such a flimsy and unsubstantial ground of hope, and the necessity of being fixed immovably on the " foundation that is laid in Zion." The young disciple, burning with all the ardour of a first affection, was thus taught the necessity of being equipped for work and warfare, and of providing against the day of trial and temptation by a familiar acquaintance with the stable and sustaining verities of the written Word of God.

From the statements kindly supplied me I select the following narrative by the Rev. William Johnston of Townsend Street church, more especially as the cases detailed are typical in their character:—

" The classes in my congregation, I should suppose, like any other, consist of the profane, the careless, the formalists, the backsliders, and the children of God. These have all been brought, more or less, under the baptism of the Holy Spirit, and effects have been produced, the personal knowledge of which has created the deep-seated and deliberate conviction, that, however many may doubt or deride, ' this is the finger of God.'

The Fallen.—" The most hopeless class in our community is composed of those who have lost the virtue and the dignity of women, and who have sunk to the lowest level of degradation which any human creature can occupy. And yet, as in the days of our Lord, harlots are entering into the kingdom of heaven before some of our wretched and lifeless Pharisees. One humble but devoted Christian woman, a member of my church, has been honoured of God to rescue, during the last few months, some twenty ' unfortunates ' out of sin and misery ; and one of the most difficult, as well as the most delightful portions of my ministerial work during the past summer has been to provide temporary support and permanent employment for those who, like the prodigal, were disposed to return. With the exception of one or two who have relapsed, by the treachery and diabolism of their own relatives and companions in crime, they are all doing admirably. Some are in good service ; one has been married ; and the rest are happy in active daily labour. Not the least interesting portion of our worshipping assembly on each Sabbath-day, and at our weekly prayer-meetings, are these Maries of the Church—these daughters of the revival—whose simple dress, marked attention, regular attendance, and steady walk, indicate the dawn of a brighter day, the foretaste of a better future.

" *The Careless* have been generally awakened ; and in *many* cases, though not in all, or perhaps in most, the work of deep conviction has issued in saving conversion. In this class ' the bodily manifestations ' seem to have been especially blessed. These manifestations have been far too much talked about, and regarded by many at a distance as if they formed the whole work, or the principal feature of it. This is a great mistake. In our congregation, there were not many cases of the kind ; but such as did occur, served, to my certain knowledge, very much the purpose of ' the rushing mighty wind ' preceding the outpouring of the Holy Spirit on the day of Pentecost. They roused the slumbering mass ; they startled whole streets ; they called special attention to the deep conviction of the person affected ; they awed and awakened the minds of many whom curiosity had brought ' to come and see ' ; and they were overruled to send many back to their homes and closets to think of their own lives, to cry to God for their own souls, and to look to Christ for pardon and acceptance as they had never looked before. Of the many illustrative cases I might quote, I shall give but few :—

"One fine but thoughtless girl, a pupil in the Sabbath-school, was asked to go and sing in the house where another person was in deep distress. She had not been many minutes in the room when the bodily manifestations so impressed her, that she went home to consider the question, ' Have I not as much reason to weep for my own sins, and pray for my own soul ? ' For days and weeks she continued in the deepest anxiety of mind, until, after a painful and protracted conflict, in which her judgment had wellnigh given way, she shut herself up to closet prayer with God, until she found peace in the finished work and perfect righteousness of Christ. She is now a consistent member of the church, and an efficient teacher in the Sabbath-school, and these exercises of her mind have been blessed to the conversion of her sister, who is also adorning the doctrine of God her Saviour.

" At the first prayer meeting in my church which returning strength permitted me to attend, when leading in the first prayer, one of my petitions was that God would be pleased to convince and convert some poor careless sinner present. Immediately after, there burst forth a most piteous, plaintive cry for mercy. The person was carried out, and the prayer proceeded, when, shortly after, another cry was heard, and another person was taken away in charge of the elders of the church. When the services in the church were concluded, I went to the school-room to speak to these persons, and, to my surprise, I found that the first affected was one of the most hardened and apparently hopeless cases in the congregation. She was a grandmother, a strong-minded, active, worldly woman—one upon whom I had been calling for twelve years, and trying, without any success, to bring to a sense of sin or to the house of God. She seemed utterly indifferent to the salvation of her soul, and twice dead in sin. On the week before, her daughter had been awakened, and she had prevailed on her poor mother to come down that evening to the prayer-meeting, and then and there she was cut to the heart. 'That's me!' she exclaimed, and a sense of her sin burst upon her mind, under which she felt utterly overpowered. Her daughter and she are both rejoicing in Jesus, and are one with Christ in the fellowship of the church.

"At our communion in October, one person came forward and asked admission to the fellowship of the church, who had been for above twenty years a seat-holder. He was an honest, good-natured, worldly, godless man, and the father of a large family. His son had been awakened, and was also asking admission. The work of grace in the heart of his child had struck home conviction to his own soul; and with a most ingenuous confession of his sin, and a powerful statement of the thorough disgust and dread with which the manifold inconsistencies of others professing religion had often filled him, he told us how the love of Christ had been shed abroad in his heart, and that he now unreservedly 'yielded himself to the Lord.' With him were seated twelve others, advanced in years, formerly careless and dead, but now humble followers of Christ, and seeking, through His mediation, admission to the fellowship of the church. Their deep sense of sin, their humbling view of self, their strong confidence in Christ, and their clear views of truth were such that they were all welcomed into the fellowship of the church, and hailed as blessed fruits of the revival. Two of the men had been for years given greatly to drink, but they are now sober and consistent Christians, and stand out monuments of sovereign grace.

The Formalists.—" Like most of my brethren in the ministry, I had too many in my church, who, whilst steady in their attendance on the means of grace, were, after all, but formalists in religion. Upon many of these the most marked change has taken place, and, as they themselves declare, 'they never knew or felt the power or peace of religion before.' One man up in years, moral in his character and well acquainted with the Word, whilst returning from the prayer-meeting in the Botanic Gardens, heard a number of lads singing one of our beautiful psalms; God ordered that sound to reach his heart, and the deepest conviction seized upon his soul. I never saw or met with a more distressed mind. He had no rest day or night for weeks. He happened to meet me one day in one of the most crowded thoroughfares of Belfast, and stopped me to ask, 'What must I do to be saved? I have been a hypocrite and a formalist for nearly forty years; I have been walking through life with a veil over my eyes, and I feel such a burden of sin, that if I do not get relief I must die, and be damned.'

For weeks no promise could give him peace. He knew his Bible well, but that only added aggravation to his guilt. Human counsels were utterly powerless. I could only pray with him, and for him. Nor was this in vain. I met him one day, and was delighted to see at once a gladsome countenance, the index of a blessed change. He told me God had shown him his mistake. He had wished God to *mend* his heart, but that would not do; and it was not until, on his knees, he had unreservedly resigned himself to the Lord, and asked the Holy Spirit to renew him in the whole man after the image of God, that the Lord Jesus had mercy on him, and had pardoned and accepted him. . . . It so happened, that a few weeks after, I began my pastoral visitation for this winter with my friend John. When seated together at his fireside, he said, ' I think, Mr Johnston, the ministers are all *preaching* a great deal better than they used to do.' ' Perhaps,' said I, ' the people are *hearing* a good deal better than they used to do.' ' That may be,' he replied; ' but I think they *ought* to preach a good deal better.' ' Why so?' I asked. ' Because,' said he, ' the people are all praying now for their ministers; and before this revival, they left all the praying as well as the preaching to them.' John is now a living stone in the spiritual temple.

"One other illustrative case is that of a young man, who, like Saul, stands out head and shoulders above most of his brethren; that fine manly body is the tenement of a clear mind and a generous disposition. He has maintained an excellent character, and is a person of very active habits. He has been for years a member of the church. He has been engaged in the spirit trade, and managed his business with all due regard to propriety, and as well as that branch of business can be conducted.

During last spring, a sermon which I preached on the sin and shame of the trade, so 'nettled' him, that for weeks and months he never entered our church. During last summer, the Spirit began to work deeply on his mind. The first serious awakening was at a prayer-meeting in Townsend Street, on an evening when a noble-minded elder of the Presbyterian Church, and a leading merchant in our town, was expounding the parable of the prodigal son. Reflection deepened into conviction, and that conviction, for several days and nights, was exhibited in agonising wrestling with God for mercy. That heavenly Father, who never said to any of the seed of Jacob, ' Seek ye my face in vain,' heard his prayer, and, after a most anxious ordeal, granted him pardon and peace through the blood of the Lamb. At one of our prayer-meetings he came forward and asked liberty to speak a few words. This granted, he proceeded to give us a most interesting statement of the rise and progress of religion in his soul. He told us that for years he had been a professor of religion, but only a formalist and a hypocrite—that he had never known what the peace of God was until within the last few days—and that if all there but knew the blessedness of religion, they would seek it at once in and through Jesus Christ, and they would not be disappointed. After an earnest appeal, he resumed his seat. Many, who had not much faith in the revival, remarked, that the address was all very well, but they would wait to see what of the whisky-shop. They had not to wait long ; the very next week the house was cleared of every vestige of the whisky trade ; he had washed his hands clear of all inconsistency ; he takes an active part in our religious meetings ; his new business prospers beyond all expectation, under the blessing of God ; he has just passed through a fearful ordeal of illness, rejoicing in tribulation; he has been the honoured instrument of bringing several of his relatives and friends to a saving knowledge of Jesus Christ, and he is going steadily forward adorning in his daily walk the doctrine of God his Saviour.

"*The Backsliders* have not been forgotten by our gracious God. Of many I might report with holy joy, but one case only will I quote. He was a young man of prepossessing appearance, excellent character, reflecting habits, and religious profession. He was well educated in the Scriptures, and much liked. He was a successful Sabbath-school teacher, and a regular communicant in the church. After some time, he was appointed superintendent of a Sabbath-school, and all went on well under his management. By-and-by a striking change passed over him. He became dissatisfied with everything, and gave up the charge of the school—fell away from the communion of the church, and finally ceased to attend the house of God. The secret of all was, he had begun to read infidel books, by which his faith was overthrown, and he was unfortunately drawn into the darkness of Deism, and openly avowed his contempt of Christianity. In this state of mind he continued for several months. When the Spirit of God visited our town and congregation, the manifestations of His power were treated by him with utter incredulity, and the whole movement was regarded as woman's weakness and nervous sympathy. The work of grace was denied; and when on one occasion the conversation turned on the power of prayer, that power was defied.—' Let any six men try and pray me down.' One humble fellow-workman, himself awakened at a prayer-meeting, and a reclaimed backslider, and at that very time anxiously alive about his own soul, secretly accepted the challenge. There was one other heart which loved that erring brother through and through—a friend who had rejoiced in his rise, and now grieved over his fall,—one who, ' since the day he heard it, did not cease to pray for him, and to desire that he might be filled with the knowledge of His will in all wisdom and spiritual understanding.' Whilst the prayers were being presented, the last case which I have detailed occurred, and that address at our prayer-meeting was reported to him by his companion. It was on a Saturday morning, and the earnest tone of that working-man, himself a monument of mercy, went to the heart of his erring friend. He went home that day in silent anxiety, and reached his home to retire at once to his closet. He took down his neglected Bible, and opening it at random, his eye fell on the 51st Psalm, and as he read it he wondered. He closed it, and opening it again, his attention was drawn to the 39th Psalm, with all its solemn warnings. Melted down, he fell on his knees, and casting himself on God in Christ for forgiveness and acceptance, all his difficulties vanished, he could not tell how, and there was no objection urged by Tom Paine to which he could not have given a sufficient answer. The next Sabbath he was at church both morning and evening; and after the conclusion of the latter service, I invited any that were anxious about their souls to meet me in the vestry. About thirty came, of whom our friend was one. My heart bounded with joy as I took his hand and brought him into the vestry, where he told us the history of his fall, and how, in the bitterness of his hatred of Christ and Christianity, he had gone to school to learn grammar and penmanship, that he might be prepared to do his best to write down religion, and how, in the manner above described, he was brought back to the Shepherd and Bishop of his soul. After this statement we all knelt together around the throne of grace, and thanked God that this His son, who was dead, was alive again, was lost, and was found. He continues a humble follower of Christ,

"In relation to the *Children of God*, they, too, have been wondrously and blessedly revived. The first case of prostration which occurred in our congregation was one of my Sabbath-school teachers, a young man of quiet, consistent Christian character. I was for some time perplexed as to the reason of his being 'struck down,' but in a short time I found that with that visitation a most remarkable stimulus had been given to his mental powers and spiritual graces—that what Mr North very properly describes as 'the dumb devil,' which possesses too many professing Christians, was thus thoroughly cast out of him—that those lips which shame and fear had sealed, were opened—and that, like Saul, he stood forth a new man under the baptism of the Spirit, which he was thus led to seek and receive. He now leads in prayer when asked, which he would not or could not do before, and is the active superintendent of one of our Sabbath-schools, besides being generally useful in the visitation of the careless and the sick. He stands out the type of a large number, whose dormant energies have been thoroughly awakened and vigorously enlisted in the cause of Christ.

"Some may deny the work of the Spirit, and some require the test of time. I can only say, that whilst a large amount of mere emotion has arisen and passed away, and whilst many have been awakened but not converted, many, very many, remain to testify to the saving work of grace which has passed upon them. Not one of those joining the church has lapsed into carelessness or inconsistency, but all stand fast in the Lord and in the power of His might."

Having had an opportunity on several occasions of hearing addresses by those who were designated as "converts," I may take the opportunity of stating, that whilst fully sensible of the value of their services, and believing that they were eminently instrumental in spreading abroad the holy flame by which both town and country were overspread, I am not less convinced that there was in many instances a very exaggerated estimate of their competency and qualifications for addressing public assemblies. So long as they confined themselves to a declaration of " the great things which the Lord had done " for them, simply narrating their own experience, and testifying to the wondrous grace and mercy they had found, their statements were invested with a peculiar and even tender interest, while their importunate pleadings with their fellow-men to accept the great salvation were fitted to come home to the heart with an unwonted power. But when they undertook to become expositors and preachers of the word, they utterly failed. How could it be otherwise ? Who could expect of uneducated youths, however piously affected, any other than the crudest statements of the gospel scheme ? unless, indeed, they were to be regarded as the subjects of an immediate revelation, their speech and even presence being endowed with all the potency of a miraculous agency.

The awakening had not visited Belfast for many weeks until some curious physical phenomena, in addition to those by which it was characterised at the outset, began to attract attention. Nor were these peculiar to the movement in any one place—they manifested themselves in several districts. I allude to the occasional suspension of the bodily powers, as indicated by the loss of speech, sight, and hearing; the subjects of them affected as in a trance—deaf, dumb, blind, and motionless—while they would frequently fall into a sleep, in which they continued for hours, and the commencement and termination of which they intimated beforehand to the bystanders.

Much injury, however, was done by the encouragement of this class of "manifestations." Those who experienced them were run after as a wonder, and their announcements treasured up as though they were the immediate product of inspiration. Attention was diverted from the essentials of the great work to some of its most painful accompaniments; and there was cause seriously to apprehend that in some instances the bodily disease thus generated so far extended its sad influence as to overshadow altogether religious impressions. I shall refer hereafter to cases in which, by the judicious interference of ministers and others, the "sleepers" were effectually awoke out of their cherished slumbers. Meanwhile it is enough to state that the phenomena in question had nothing either of miracle or mystery about them, but may be explained by the laws which regulate the action of the mental on the material frame. All these deplorable attendants on the movement, however, have long since passed away; while a healthier state of public feeling in regard to such affections now happily prevails over the entire community.

Respecting the extent of the movement in Belfast, I may observe that although many in different districts were brought under its influence, yet, in a community consisting of at least 120,000, of whom there were tens of thousands, both Roman Catholic and others, of the lowest grade in point of intellectual and moral culture, it was not to be expected that such a change would be effected as would sensibly elevate the character of the general population—especially of that class which, in our great towns and cities, so largely contributes to swell the records of vice and crime.

8

The Revival Around Belfast

" WHEN the Lord is about to visit a neighbourhood in mercy," says the Rev. Joseph Barkley, of Carnmoney, " He usually puts it into His people's hearts to pray for it. It was so here—for having heard what the Lord was doing in other places, a deep anxiety pervaded every bosom that we should not be passed by ; and although there were no formal concerts for prayer, there was many a praying Jacob, in the family and in the closet, wrestling for a blessing. The answer was not long delayed, but it came in a way none of us had anticipated. A Christian merchant from Belfast, on the first Sabbath in June, felt *constrained*, as he said himself, though *unsolicited*, to come out and address us on the subject of revivals, and to tell us more especially of what he had himself witnessed of the Lord's doings on the previous night ; and although therewas nothing in his address, so far as man could judge, calculated to produce an impression, yet that evening two females, in their own houses, were in deep distress about their souls, accompanied by great bodily weakness. A few evenings after, the same gentleman addressed an immense meeting in the church, and never perhaps was there a more striking illustration of the words, ' Not by might or by power, but by my Spirit, saith the Lord.' For barely had he spoken ten sentences, and these not remarkable for power or persuasiveness, or anything of the kind, when one and another were ' stricken down,' crying to the Lord for mercy; and then the glory of the Lord so filled the house that it became a literal Bochim, and before morning it was computed that not less than fifty souls had found peace in believing. Never can that night be forgotten here. A few weeks later our communion was held; and on the evening following, so glorious was the manifestation of the Spirit's presence and power that upwards of one hundred may be said to have been brought to Christ from one meeting alone. It is indeed 'a night to be long remembered' in this place; day had dawned before the last of the stricken ones had found peace; and in the calm of a summer morning the songs of thanksgiving were heard for miles, as happy bands of rejoicing believers wended their way homewards, praising God for His mercy; and if there was joy on earth, higher far was the joy in heaven over those repenting sinners returning to the Lord.

"Before that week had closed, multitudes of strong young men and women from among the farming population were gathered to Christ, and nothing was more common than to hear of numbers finding peace in their own homes. In several instances the day-schools had to be dismissed, in consequence of the children being 'stricken down'; while, in one case, an entire school, even while attending to the secular department of the business, was literally prostrated, and one-half of the children, say from thirty to forty, are now rejoicing in Christ. Strong men who looked upon that scene wept outright; and few could hear these children pray, after they had found peace, without feeling that the Spirit was poured out upon them of a truth. The work is still progressing steadily, though in a more silent and imperceptible manner than heretofore. Rarely a week passes that I do not hear of one or more conversions; and I am confident I no not exaggerate when I say (and to God be all the glory !) that within the bounds of this congregation alone not fewer than from three to four hundred souls profess to have found peace during the past six or eight months. It is a cause of much thankfulness to be enabled further to state that, without almost an exception, their ' conversation is such as becometh the gospel of Christ.'

A marked and marvellous change is now visible over the entire district. Twenty prayer-meetings are held weekly, where not one was in existence before. Mere factory lads and girls are holding concerts for prayer. A short time ago one of the little fellows came to me, saying, " See, sir, this is my comrade in the mill ; I have *prayed him out*, and he is now rejoicing with me.' Those who have found Christ themselves are most anxious to bring others to Him ; and hence, whilst teachers for our Sabbath-schools could not be had some time ago, there is no lack of them at present. There is an air of spiritual beauty now resting on the moral landscape here that is quite refreshing. Total abstinence is the order of the day. Even moderate drinking has all but disappeared ; while drunkenness, except in the case of a few old topers, is altogether unknown ; and even of the most confirmed of them we do not despair, as God has already plucked many such out of the fire. The line of demarcation betwixt the Church and the world is now marked and distinct. Torpor has given place to activity ; the stillness and malaria of the stagnant pool to the rushing of the waters of life."

A few miles distant from the place last noticed is Ballycarry, of which the Rev. John Stuart writes as follows :—

" Here was erected the first Presbyterian church in Ireland. Here the Rev. Edward Brice, in 1613, unfurled the banner of Scotland's covenant, and began preaching the everlasting gospel. Two faithful and godly ministers were his successors, and then for eighty long years the church lay under the incubus of Arianism—the frozen zone of Christianity. The God, however, who reserved to Himself seven thousand souls who had not bowed the knee to the image of Baal, reserved here a goodly remnant which adhered to the Synod of Ulster when, in 1829, their minister and a portion of his flock openly abandoned the faith of God's people. Since that time, our church, like the house of David, has waxed stronger and stronger, and '*Unitarianism,*' as the heresy is now called, like the house of Saul, has waxed weaker and weaker, God's gracious revival which commenced early in May last, has still more added to our members. Through the mighty working of the Holy Spirit on the hearts of sinners, forty souls have been brought from under that Christless system into the communion of our church, and God has bestowed on some of them, both males and females, wonderful power of prayer and fluency of expression.

"In this extensive district God's right hand and holy arm have won many victories. Never was there such a summer as the last; never such an autumn; never such a winter, so far as it has gone. Hundreds have been savingly converted to the Lord, some 'stricken' down when the Spirit came upon them like a 'rushing mighty wind.' Others were convinced and converted whilst He spake to their consciences by the 'still small voice.' The first effect of the revival was that 'fear came upon *every soul.*' Then was our church filled to suffocation, and we were obliged to take to the open fields to declare the message of mercy to a hungering and thirsting population. The hitherto unoccupied pews were ardently sought after. All were engaged. The aisles were filled with *forms* crowded with anxious hearers, and now preaching became a luxury. I had pastor's work to do. I had living men and living women before me. They came to the sanctuary on the sole errand of obtaining the ' bread of life.' Every Sabbath was a day of sweet ' refreshing.' On every week-day evening ' they that feared the Lord spake to one another, and the Lord hearkened and heard,' and ' there were added to the church daily such as should be saved.' Of all the *stricken ones*—two hundred in number—I do not know of one backslider."

Very similar statements may be made regarding the neighbouring districts of Ballyeaston, Ballinderry, and specially Dundrod.

Before passing away from the neighbourhood of Belfast, it is necessary to advert to certain physical phenomena, of a delusive character that sprang up under the shadow of the revival, and by which for a time many were deceived. I allude to what are called the " marks," being neither less nor more than appearances on the body, resembling printed characters, impressed thereon, as it was represented, by a Divine agency. About the beginning of September these new developments began in Belfast to attract attention, and to excite the eager curiosity of the multitude. A young woman, for instance, who had been seized some three months previously, and who had been the subject of a nervous disease, aggravated by fits of dumbness and the like, would, in consequence of her repeated " prophesyings " of the further deprivations she would undergo, come to be regarded as in direct communication with heaven. By and by, however, sceptical people among the bystanders, even in her own humble circle, would begin to question her pretensions. What, then, was to be done ? How were the unbelievers to be put to silence, and the vaticinations of the pythoness to be vindicated against the gainsayers ? Why, by a notable miracle. Accordingly, strange signs would appear upon her person. Unbaring her bosom or her arm, she would exhibit to the admiring onlookers a mystic word or symbol, impressed so legibly that all might read and understand. What if the lettering were somewhat indistinct, or if the sacred name were incorrectly spelled ? For this she was in no wise accountable. She was only passive in the hand of a higher agent. All unbelief would vanish before the preternatural authentication.

The intelligence of this new phase in the movement naturally produced a wonderful sensation. Hundreds flocked to witness the extraordinary phenomenon, and though the more discriminating might shrewdly conjecture that the " marks " could be accounted for without any other than a very ordinary interposition, there was enough of credulity in the multitude to yield assent to them as the genuine operation of a Divine hand. If any questioned their existence, or, in certain cases, could not trace them out distinctly, it was " because they had not been stricken down," and therefore had not the visual organs requisite for such a delicate perception. Most of the visitors, it was remarked, were expected to pay for the gratification of their curiosity. Such instances had begun to increase and multiply to an extent which it was serious to contemplate, when public attention was directed towards them in a way that cast a new light on their character. A meeting was held one evening in the town of Lisburn for the purpose of hearing from the lips of one of the ministers (the Rev. William Breakey) a statement bearing on his investigations into these new physical appearances. After a vindication of the revival as a genuine work of the Holy Spirit, the speaker entered on an exposure of the phenomena in question, his testimony being corroborated by other witnesses. He stated, in substance, that he had personally visited the parties on whom such marks were found, and that he had no difficulty in coming to the conclusion that they were produced by some clumsy process of manipulation ; and he denounced the whole affair as an imposture, fitted only to delude the credulous, and bring discredit on the work of God. Although it required some little courage to undertake this duty, owing to the excited state of feeling among the common people, the exposure was followed by a rapid return to reason and propriety, the *furor* which so extensively prevailed upon the subject almost immediately subsided, and " the work," in that district at least, was saved the imputation of ministering to the excesses of fanaticism.

9

The Revival and the General Assembly

THE meeting of the General Assembly, which was held in the city of Dublin in the beginning of July 1859, was one of the most memorable convocations that ever came together to deliberate respecting the kingdom and work of God. Twelve months before, an unusual solemnity had prevailed during those special services in which the representatives of the Presbyterian Church were occupied in conference and prayer respecting the great revival in another land; and now that a kindred movement had commenced and spread so rapidly among themselves, it was felt on all sides that the occasion was invested with an unparalleled and pregnant interest.

The proceedings of the meeting, from the outset, were so arranged as that a prominent place was assigned to the revival movement. It was resolved accordingly that an early day should be set apart, in the first instance, for private conference, and subsequently for public recognition of this great work of God. The adoption of this course was deemed of primary importance, as the awakening was itself a new thing in the midst of us, and certain of its attendant circumstances were so peculiar as to demand the gravest consideration of the highest judicatory of the Church. It was necessary therefore that an opportunity should be afforded in private for a full statement on the part of those who were more especially conversant with the work in its characteristic aspects;

and, in the next place, that a mode of dealing with it should be adopted which could approve itself to the "collective wisdom." The conference thus entered on was felt throughout to be an eminently seasonable and edifying occasion. One after another of the members, for nearly four hours, rose in his place to contribute to the general interest, either by a narrative of what he had witnessed in his own congregation, or by the expression of a judgment in regard to what had been communicated by others.

Reference has been made, in proceeding portions of this narrative, to the visit of Mr Brownlow North, and the seasonable character of his addresses to all classes of the community. This eminent evangelist, although a member of the Episcopal Church, had at the meeting of the General Assembly of the Free Church of Scotland been publicly recognised as an honoured servant of Christ, and had been formally invited to occupy the pulpits of its ministers. Having witnessed on that occasion, in company with the Rev. Dr Johnston, then moderator of our Assembly, the very impressive exercises connected with his recognition, I took the opportunity of inviting him to visit us at the period of our annual meeting. Although he had many engagements in Scotland, Mr North acceded to our solicitations, and received a cordial greeting from our highest ecclesiastical judicatory.

In consequence of the awakening, and the desire of the great majority of the ministers to return to their respective flocks before the Sabbath, it was found necessary to adjourn the meeting before its business was more than half concluded—a circumstance which was in itself a striking attestation to the movement. And thus this memorable occasion passed. It was felt throughout that the deliberations of our Assembly were pervaded by an overawing solemnity never realised before, filling the soul with a profound sense of Jehovah's presence, subduing personal prejudices and prepossessions, and infusing a spirit of mutual forbearance and generous conciliation. The Lord had visited His Church as a court in His own house, so that, even in its ecclesiastical procedure, there had been realised as pure delight, as sweet communion, and as ennobling aspirations as could be hoped for in the most favoured times of visitation. It is impossible ever to forget those hours of blessing that flew by on rapid wing, when the theme of every tongue was the Spirit's wondrous grace and power, and when every heart was melted, as under the descent of a heavenly influence. It was with feelings such as these that the proceedings were suspended, and that the brethren returned to their several flocks.

Nearly three months after, their consultations were resumed, not on this occasion in Dublin, but in Belfast. The great effusion which before had fallen on so considerable a portion on the field had meanwhile widely extended in its range, and many who before had been in heaviness, because as yet their congregations had been unvisited by the "gracious rain," were now rejoicing in its abundant and pleasant fruits. Nor were there any indications that the clouds of heaven had exhausted their stores of blessing. Other lands had also shared the joy with which so many had been gladdened, and from the ends of the earth had arisen songs of thanksgiving for what in this far-distant isle of ocean God had wrought. The period which had elapsed since the adjournment in Dublin had furnished a more extended opportunity of testing its real character, and of forming a judgment of all its attendant features. The Church, accordingly, having discharged her primary obligation of acknowledging the favour shewn in this great work of God, it was now felt that her more immediate duty was to consider how the work itself might be directed, so that it might be preserved, as far as human effort could accomplish that result, from the weakness and fatuity of man, and from the devices of the great adversary.

As on the former occasion, a conference was held, and various resolutions were adopted—one of which was to the effect, " That the Assembly appoint a special day for public worship in all our churches, and for prayer and thanksgiving to Almighty God for His gracious mercy vouchsafed in the revival of religion ; and that supplication be offered for the extension of this gracious work to all churches and all lands ; " and further, " that our moderator be requested to prepare an address, including reasons for the observance of such day, to be printed and circulated immediately amongst the brethren."

10

The Revival and the Orangemen

FOR many years the anniversary of the Battle of the Boyne had been associated in the minds of the lower class of Irish Protestants with uncontrollable displays of party animosity and hatred. Glorious in itself as was the achievement of William of Orange in breaking the iron dominion of a Papal despot, and in erecting constitutional liberty on its ruins, that illustrious name had with the unthinking multitude become a synonym for ignorant bravado, and for unreasoning hostility both to the system and the abettors of Romanism. With the return of each successive Twelfth of July there was an ebullition of political and religious frenzy, often provocative of resistance, and terminating in violence and bloodshed.

For years there was a certain quarter in Belfast which had attained an unenviable notoriety. As the Twelfth of July drew near, it had been customary to reinforce the military and police, that they might keep the peace, if possible, beween the turbulent inhabitants of Sandy Row and the " Ribbonmen " who occupied a neighbouring district. Not only had the ordinary street missiles been flung in plentiful profusion on the scene of conflict, but deadly collisions had taken place, shots had been fired, and blood had run upon the streets. For weeks the magistrates and military were nightly on patrol. The strong arm of the executive had at length to interfere by martial law and by a disarming of the parties who had shewn that they were wholly unfit to be intrusted with arms.

"When, however, the revival was at its height," writes the Librarian of the Belfast Society, "Sandy Row was visited by persons from all parts of the country— indeed, of the kingdom. Clergymen and pious laymen were constantly holding open-air meetings; and it was on the evening of the Twelfth that I first took part in one of these. In former years it would have been no ordinary feat to have passed through some of the most intensely Popish and Orange districts of the city; but I had no fears now. There were no breaking of lamps and constables' heads—no flinging of paving stones. The streets were crowded with the young of both sexes, but the 23rd Psalm was falling in sweet cadence on the gale; and none of the usual emblems of the Twelfth appeared,—no orange garlands, no arches flung over the streets. There was no military or semi-military parade; the only peace-preserver was the usual night constable."

Visiting, in company with a friend, a short time afterwards, in a row inhabited exclusively by mill hands, and meeting a number of girls who had been brought under the influence of the revival, they all exclaimed, referring to the late anniversary, "It was another sort of Twelfth than the one before it. None of us would have wrought a turn on that day; but now we were all at our work as usual. You would not have known it was the Twelfth at all." "You may well say that," remarked one of their number, who had been, till a few weeks before, a Roman Catholic. "Don't you remember how you chased me, and others of my sort, through the country for hours that day, till you nearly frightened us out of our wits? But now we are all like sisters of one family, and the head of it is Christ."

The same testimony has been borne from other noted Orange districts, such as Lurgan, Lisburn, Dundrod, and counties Tyrone, Armagh, Derry, and Monaghan.

We do not wonder, after such records as these, that Chief Baron Pigott, himself a Roman Catholic, should have taken occasion, when sitting on the bench in County Down, a few days after the great Orange anniversary, to refer, in the language of the reporters, " to the religious movement in the north as having extinguished all party animosities, and produced the most wholesome moral results upon the community at large ; " and that he should have " expressed a hope that it would extend over the whole country, and influence society to its lowest depths."

11

The Revival in County Down

I CANNOT more appropriately introduce the narrative of the revival movement in County Down than by inserting in this place a communication with which I have been favoured on the subject by the esteemed Bishop of the diocese, Dr Knox, although part of his ecclesiastical domain lies in the County Antrim. It has been already mentioned that on an early period his lordship lent his countenance to the work, both by the sanction given to his clergy in their labours in connection therewith, and by his presence at one of the first united meetings for prayer held in Belfast. His correspondence subsequently with Bishop M'Ilvaine, of Ohio, in the United States, exhibited his anxious desire to have the sympathy of those occupying an influential position in the Episcopal Church of America, who had been familiar with the history of revivals in that land; while the prominent part he took at the Annual Conference of the Evangelical Alliance, at a still later period, when he bore emphatic testimony to the reality and good effects of the revival, sufficiently attested his appreciation of this great work of God. Knowing that in the course of the season he had directed a communication to be addressed to all the ministers in his diocese, making particular inquiry in relation to the several phases of the movement, and having had abundant experience of that courtesy and catholicity for which he is distinguished,

I took the liberty of requesting of his lordship a brief statement of the result ; and, further, desiring his permission to avail myself in the present publication of his testimony. To the request he was pleased to accede, in the following terms :—

"THE PALACE, HOLYWOOD, BELFAST,
February 13, 1860.

"MY DEAR SIR,—It affords me very great pleasure to comply with your request to furnish you with the result of some of the queries which I issued to my clergy in reference to the religious awakening, which, in the good providence of God, has visited this Province, making many a barren spot fruitful, and many a sorrowing heart glad.

"To my queries, I received from my clergy one hundred and six replies ; seventy-five of which bore the most gratifying testimony to the spiritual blessings which followed the 'revivals' in their own parishes—such as the careless aroused, the impure made pure, the drunkard reformed, the prayerless prayerful, and every means of grace eagerly attended.

"I enclose you a copy of a few of the answers which I have received to two of my queries, shewing the nature of this wonderful religious and moral reformation, and the truly spiritual character of this great work, as testified by faithful, zealous, and earnest clergymen in my diocese ; and I feel satisfied that the evidence of the clergy of your own Church, which your high official position will enable you to procure, will fully corroborate the same. To their zealous labours, also, in this our day of 'great things,' I would, in passing, pay the just tribute of sincere respect.

"I cannot conclude without mentioning the result of

my late confirmations in Belfast, as it marks the deep impression and devotional feeling which the Spirit of the living God, moving over this portion of our land, has kindled. The numbers confirmed annually by me in the parish of Belfast have averaged about two hundred and fifty, but last year they reached seven hundred and five, and never since I have administered that rite of my Church have I witnessed such solemnity of manner and deep feeling as was exhibited by all whom I then confirmed.

"And now, my dear Sir, may the word spoken by us all be blessed by God's Holy Spirit to those among whom we minister, that, in the true revival of a sanctified life, they may become 'living epistles of Christ, known and read of all men.'—Believe me, with sincere respect, yours truly and faithfully,

"ROB. DOWN & CONNOR & DROMORE.

"To the Rev. Professor Gibson."

Castlereagh is a rural district not far distant from Belfast. It was visited by the awakening soon after its manifestation in the latter place. For six years previously there was a marked improvement in spiritual things; and now that the revival has come, a great enlargement has been experienced, while no case of apostasy or backsliding is known.

The Rev. Dr Given supplies the following incidents:—

The Converted Cripple.—"Among the early cases of revival within the bounds of my congregation was a cripple, who had been in the habit of visiting the various places to which his business led him, by means of a donkey-cart, though he could not be persuaded to use the same mode of conveyance to bring him to the house of God. Many a time as I met him by the way, or found

THE REVIVAL IN COUNTY DOWN

him in his own house, I had endeavoured to prevail on him to attend public worship, but was usually met with the same stereotyped excuses,—his lameness, the awkwardness of the thing, the inconvenience it would cause himself, and the trouble it might occasion others. In vain did I labour to remove such pretexts, and urge on him the importance of making at least an equal effort to come to the sanctuary as to reach the place of business. He could attend to the perishing interests of the present passing world, while to the realities of a future and a better he remained utterly indifferent. Years of carelessness rolled away. Conscience would sometimes trouble him, but he soon quieted it. The thought that God, in depriving him of the use of his limbs, had exonerated him from attendance on His service, would from time to time silence the still small voice within, and confirm him in his guilty neglect. At length he was apprehended of Christ, and arrested in his course. He had heard of the revival in the neighbouring county, and talked of it as a matter of news with others. He had been attending no religious meeting, hearing no gospel sermon, nor listening to any stirring address; but one night, on retiring to rest, the Spirit of God brought his sins very vividly before his mind, and putting the desire in his heart, and the words in his mouth, constrained him to cry aloud, and for some time continue to cry, 'Lord, be merciful to me a sinner.' He remained under deep convictions of sin till the Sabbath following, when, to the amazement of neighbours and acquaintances, he was seen approaching the house of God. The sermon that day was blessed to him; and that same Sabbath night, after much wrestling earnest prayer, deep agony, and many tears, he obtained the peace that passeth understanding. Since then he has possessed new light, new life, new love; and not one Sabbath since have I missed him from his accustomed place in the house of God. Great has been his joy in believing; his conduct and conversation also have been most consistent. He loses no opportunity of testifying for God, and recommending to others the Saviour whom he himself has found. As his change was a marvel to many at the time it occurred, so has his behaviour ever since been truly an ensample, and himself a living epistle, seen and read of all. From Sabbath to Sabbath he is carried in and out of my church, without ever breathing an excuse, or hinting a difficulty, or uttering a complaint in regard to his infirmity, but grateful to the kind friends who are ever ready to attend to him; and rejoicing in God his Saviour, he goes on his way, feeling by personal experience, and practically illustrating the truth, that wherever there is a will to serve the Lord there is sure to be a way.

The Formalist.—" A second instance of the reviving grace of God is that of a female, who had from early youth attended the house of God with regularity, and who had often partaken of the Supper of the Lord. Still she had only the form of godliness, and wanted the living power. She had never closed with Christ, though she had united herself to His people. She had often thought of death, and always with alarm. The consideration of her latter end, which often forced itself upon her, filled her with terror. To her those words of Scripture literally applied—' Through fear of death' she had been 'all her life subject to bondage.' At length deliverance came. It is a pleasant Sabbath morning in the month of August; the sky is clear, the air balmy, and the fields waving with golden grain. Little groups of worshippers are leisurely wending their way to ' the church that crowns the neighbouring hill,' and the individual referred to is among them. What with the mildness of the weather, the scenery around, the companions by the way, her heart was lighter, and her thoughts more cheerful than usual. Arrived in the sanctuary, there was nothing that interested her more than on other occasions, till the announcement of the text. It was contained in the words, ' Remember Lot's wife,' chosen as the groundwork of remarks which I deemed suitable to be addressed to the many in connection with my congregation, who, I knew, had been recently the subjects of a saving change, and whom I was anxious to warn against looking back after having put their hand to the plough, or turning back to the old ways of sin and death. The text at once riveted her attention, and as the sermon proceeded, her memory reverted to the sins and faults of youth, the inconsistencies of riper years, the hollowness of outward profession without inward principle or corresponding practice. A burden pressed sore upon her heart. Tears flowed copiously and, mingled with big drops of perspiration, wetted the shawl that lay around her shoulders. She felt extremely weak, but, anxious to escape observation, made an effort to get out of the church. She had only succeeded in leaving the pew when I observed her face become deadly pale, and she sank apparently unconscious in the aisle. It was no fainting fit, as she has positively and repeatedly assured me since. At the close of the service, and during prayer with her, she thought she saw the Saviour, clothed in a white garment reaching down to the feet, approach her. Be that as it may, one thing is certain, she has found the Lord, the fear of death has been removed, the Word of God is understood and appreciated by her as it had never been before. Her life, at the same time, as far as I have been able to judge, is in perfect harmony with the change."

The neighbourhood of Comber was the very earliest visited by the revival in the county in which it is situated. For about fourteen years previously, meetings had been held for the purpose of seeking a revival of religion, and when the Spirit at length came upon the people, it was with wondrous power. Hundreds were awakened and savingly turned to God.

Extent and Power of the Revival in First Comber.—" Our congregation," says the Rev. J. M. Killen, " having been the first in County Down blessed with the outpouring of the Spirit when the work commenced, a great sensation was produced. The whole town and neighbourhood were roused. Many did not retire to rest the first night at all, and for several days great numbers were unable to attend to their usual avocations, but gave themselves almost unceasingly to the study of the Scriptures, singing and prayer; and for the first month, with about three exceptions, I did not get to bed till morning, such was the anxiety of the people for pastoral instruction and consolation. For twenty-one days after the revival commenced we had on an average more than *ten* cases daily, and altogether we have had above three hundred and fifty cases of visible awakening in our congregation, not to speak of the still more numerous instances of a silent character, of which no proper estimate can yet be formed. The revival, too, has embraced those hitherto beyond the pale of the church altogether; and drunkards have been reformed, prostitutes reclaimed, thieves have become honest—Sabbath-breakers, profane swearers, scoffers, neglecters of ordinances, and worthless characters of all descriptions have been awakened or converted. No sex or age has been exempt. Our converts include children of seven and old men and women of upwards of seventy years of age. Those renewed, too,

THE REVIVAL IN COUNTY DOWN 117

especially the females, manifest a wonderful power in prayer and fluency of expression, and as yet I know no case of apostasy amongst them.

Mr Killen gives a number of interesting incidents, which, however, are so similar to others reported in other pages, that lack of space prevents their insertion.

A few miles from Comber is Killinchy, celebrated as the scene of the faithful labours of Livingstone, one of the early fathers of the Presbyterian Church. This parish during the summer months was largely visited by the reviving influence. The Hon. and Rev. Henry Ward, for thirty-five years revered as one of the most devoted ministers of the Establishment, and rector of the parish, co-operated throughout with the Rev. David Anderson, the Presbyterian minister, " the labour being divided," to use his own words, " between the ministers of the two denominations, no distinction being made, and the hearts of all knit together in one holy bond of Christian fellowship." From a letter, dated March 31, 1860, addressed by him to the Bishop of Down, I am permitted to give the following statement with reference to the results in that wide district :—

" I am happy to inform your Lordship that, from my own experience, as well as from the testimony of the Presbyterian minister with whom I have been associated, more particularly in the revival work, most satisfactory fruits have followed the wide-spread confession of sin and profession of repentance which attended the ministrations of the gospel during last summer in this neighbourhood. We might reasonably have expected to hear of many cases of relapse, and in some quarters of a reaction, during the winter season, when all extra meetings had to a considerable extent been suspended, and all physical manifestations had disappeared; but nothing of the kind has reached our ears. The extreme vigilance and jealousy of some who have watched the progress of the work more closely, have led them to fear the stability of one or two who made a profession; but this only proves that if any cases had occurred calculated to throw discredit on the work, it could not have escaped observation. Weekly prayer-meetings are very generally held over the whole parish, conducted by laymen of piety and discretion, and are very well attended, and daily family worship is continued in houses where, up to the revival movement, utter ungodliness prevailed."

In no part of the province, so far as I can learn, has there been a more genuine work of grace than in the town of Newtownards. The following statement in regard to it has been furnished by Mr M. Harrison, the intelligent teacher of the National School in that place who has had much to do in connection with the revival, although he refers to his own labours in such a modest way that it is sometimes difficult to identify them :—

State of Religion Previously.—" Before giving you an account of the work of the Lord here, it is necessary that I should tell you something regarding the state of the town previous to that blessed awakening. Our population is about twelve thousand, and we are supplied with four congregations in connection with the General Assembly, two Covenanting, two Methodist, and one Established Church. There is also a congregation of Unitarians, and one of Roman Catholics. The attendance on all these did not amount to more than twelve hundred persons on an average, and of these a considerable number came from the country districts around. From statistics made out by our town missionary, we came to the conclusion that fully one-half of the population had not even a nominal connection with any place of worship. You will see from this that religion was in a very low state among us, and you will not be surprised to hear that this town supported some seventy public-houses and more than a dozen pawn-shops. Their necessary pendants, Sabbath desecration, intemperance, and immorality were fearfully prevalent.

"Such was the state of things about the 1st of May last. Some time previous to this, the attention of many had been directed to the accounts of the marvellous work that the Lord was doing in Connor, Ahoghill, and other places in Antrim. A school-master, a native of that district, went down to see for himself the wondrous things about which he had heard so much. The reality exceeded the fame, and he came back deeply convinced that the finger of God alone could produce what he had seen. He engaged two young men—one a teacher, and the other a Scripture reader—to come to Newtownards and give an account of what the Lord was doing around them. They came about a week after, and before a considerable audience gave a narrative of the wondrous scenes they had witnessed. Many seemed deeply impressed; others were sceptical, on account of the physical accompaniments. They wished for a revival, but were not reconciled to the *modus operandi* of the Holy Spirit. I should state that, about a week before the arrival of the young men, a united prayer-meeting had been established on Wednesday evening, which was to be continued weekly. It commenced in one of the Covenanting churches, and was attended by about two hundred persons. This number, though but small, was looked upon by every one as something marvellous. One of our most popular divines could hardly have drawn together such an audience on a week-day evening a month previously. This prayer-meeting was changed from house to house, until it had gone over all the evangelical churches in the town, the audience gradually increasing. Still, few but church-goers attended. The vast outlying population had yet to be reached—*the lost* were yet to be sought and saved. For this purpose the Spirit used His own instruments; and, in order that He might have all the glory, they were weak ones.

The Schoolmaster turned Preacher.—" On the Lord's-day after the visit of the young men, the schoolmaster, (Mr H.) who had invited them, was much pressed in spirit by observing the Sabbath desecration which was so prevalent in the street in which he lived. It was a lovely evening, and the people were spending it standing idly at their doors, talking about the world and things thereof —their children, meanwhile, playing noisily before their eyes. Both young and old seemed to have forgotten that their Creator had ever commanded them to keep His day holy. Mr H. went out about half-past six P.M., and called on a number of the people, inviting them to come to his schoolroom at seven o'clock, as he wished to talk and pray with them. Among others, he visited the bellman of the town, notorious for his drunkenness and profligacy. Many of them promised to attend; but after waiting half-an-hour-beyond the appointed time, only *two children made their appearance!* It suddenly occurred to Mr H. that if they would not come in to hear him, it was his duty to go out and speak to them; and although unaccustomed to public speaking, and naturally of a timid disposition, he felt he was moved by an impulse which he could not resist. He went out to a place where two streets crossed, opened his Bible, and commenced to sing a psalm. The novelty of the preacher, who was well

THE REVIVAL IN COUNTY DOWN

known to the people, drew together in a few minutes more than a hundred persons. Mr H. addressed them from the parable of the barren fig-tree (Luke xiii. 6-9). The speaker was helped wonderfully, and all seemed deeply impressed. One heart at least was opened to attend to the things that were spoken, that of the drunken bellman, who, to the surprise of all, was present. He did not cry out at the meeting, nor was he prostrated, but for some days after he could neither eat nor sleep. He was in darkness and in heaviness; a strange weight pressed upon his soul; a yearning for something, such as he had never felt before, occupied all his thoughts. A few evenings after, Mr H. asked him out to take a walk with him, and then he told him of the love of Jesus, and that He had died to save him. The man stopped, and lifted up his hands in an ecstasy of joy. The darkness and the heaviness had vanished, and a flood of light, love, and peace, filled his soul. Ten months have since elapsed, but J. K. still continues steadfast. Although often tempted by his former wicked companions, he never since has entered a public-house. Under his humble roof, which once resounded with oaths and imprecations, a family altar has been erected, upon which is daily offered that sacrifice which is never despised when presented by our great High Priest. Instead of abusing his wife and children, as was formerly the case, he is now a kind husband and father; and whoever is absent from church or prayer-meeting, J. K. is sure to be in his place. Such, as far as known to us, are the first-fruits of the revival in Newtownards.

The Work Spreads.—" The open-air meeting, so auspiciously begun, was continued from Sabbath to Sabbath in the same place. The attendance rapidly increased, until, instead of hundreds, thousands were present. About three weeks after it commenced, the Scripture-reader before mentioned had been appointed to the situation of town missionary. He was asked to address this meeting. As he had come from the district where the revival had made most progress, and as his labours had been greatly blessed, there was much anxiety to hear him, and the meeting was a large one. A young woman, whose clothing was so deficient that she could not go out to the street, heard him from the window. The Spirit carried the word in power to her heart, and she was deeply convinced of sin. She rose from her seat, got down on her knees beside her loom— she was a weaver—and cried, in a most heartrending tone, 'God be merciful to me a sinner'; 'Lord save me.' She remained in this position for the greater part of the night. The house was crowded with anxious faces. Sin and salvation seemed to be the all-pervading subjects of thought with every one present. How to escape the one and obtain the other, was the inquiry of many hearts. One man present—a soldier, and a Unitarian—was observed with the tears trickling down his cheeks. The work had now fairly commenced, and during the week it spread rapidly. A considerable number of similar cases of awakening occurred in almost every street in the town. Among others, a number of prostitutes were convinced of sin, and were heard crying for mercy. The public excitement was great. Every face wore an expression of awe. In thousands of hearts, and on hundreds of lips, was the question, 'What must I do to be saved?' On Wednesday evening, the largest church in the town was crowded, ground-floor and gallery, pews and aisles. Hundreds could not get admission, and would not go away. The lawn in front of the church was densely filled; some one in the crowd gave out a psalm; and

THE REVIVAL IN COUNTY DOWN

prayer and praise ascended to the throne of God from the outside as well as from the inside of the church. More than four thousand persons must have been present at that prayer-meeting.

"The sale of religious tracts and books, but especially of Bibles, was greatly increased. Parcel after parcel was obtained from Belfast, hundreds of copies were sold, and hundreds were given gratis to those who were unable to purchase. A society also was organised for the purpose of leaving a tract monthly at every house in the town.

"The revival is now ten months old among us, so that we have ample time to test its results. The excitement has passed away, but the great majority of the awakened manifest, by a 'life and conversation becoming the gospel,' that they have indeed 'passed from death unto life.' Those who were merely frightened into a temporary sobriety, have, as might be expected, returned to their old habits, and in consequence the haunts of vice have rallied a little; but after making deductions for all this, there is much cause for thankfulness to the Father of mercies for the abundant shower of Divine grace with which we have been visited."

12

The Revival in County Down
(Continued)

ONE Sabbath evening in the end of June I had an opportunity of witnessing the first-fruits of revival in the County Down.

On alighting at the manse of Broadmills I was met by the Rev. G. H. Shanks with a joyous congratulation. The revival had come a few days before, and his countenance was lighted up with an expression of mingled gratitude and joy. The whole " country side " was now in movement. I could have learned what had taken place by the crowds of earnest men and women through which I passed, all with their Bibles in their hands, and indicating that they were converging to some common place of meeting. On the morning before, I was informed by Mr Shanks, so many as seventy under deep soul-concern were at the manse by ten o'clock, while all night long the house was filled with persons who had been taken there after the meetings of the evening. Then as we walked along to the church, the pastor pointed to this and that dwelling as having been the scene of a wondrous visitation within the last few days, old things having passed away, and all things become new.

At the church it was almost impossible to effect an entrance. Never had such an assemblage been collected there, and never had the community around been stirred by such a profound and general interest. The numbers

THE REVIVAL IN COUNTY DOWN

were so great that it was evident they could not be accommodated in one place, and so an extra service was conducted in the school-house by the Rev. Alexander Dobbin. On ascending the pulpit I endeavoured to suit my discourse to their existing state and feelings, opening up and pressing home the unconditional freeness of the gospel of Christ. As I proceeded, there was profound solemnity and intense emotion, and one or two occasionally quietly retired; but there were no prostrations, such as usually were exhibited on such occasions. At the close, and after the benediction, nearly all remained, and, breaking up into groups, fell into earnest conversation, or, gathering around some friend or neighbour who had given signs of mental distress, engaged in prayer or praise. Many were there who had found peace on the preceding evenings, and who were testifying to others the overflowing fulness of their joy. A countryman and his wife, both of whom had been the subjects of the gracious visitation, left the place with an enlargement of heart unfelt before, and as they went, they sang together one of the songs of Zion. Here was a knot of young women, who had not seen each other since they had been severally brought to Christ, and as they met, they literally rushed into each other's arms. There was a group of boys clasped in affectionate embraces, while one was saying, "Precious Jesus!" another, "Oh, that all would come to Him!" a third, "He is the chief among ten thousand, and altogether lovely!" while another still, in the fervour of his new-born love, was moving about among those present on the green, and saying, "Look to Jesus all of you—look, and live!" Hard by were some silent weepers, and one or two who were labouring in sore agony, as though all the waves of Divine wrath were raging round and over them. It was a scene ever to be remembered by those who witnessed it—a marvellous manifestation of the love of God the Father, the grace of the Lord Jesus Christ, and the communion of the Holy Spirit.

These beginnings, so full of promise, were succeeded by other incidents of like interest; and in no district was the work more entirely in accordance with that sobriety and order which are so desirable in a time of general excitement. I shall allow Mr Shanks himself to continue and conclude the narrative:—" For some five weeks, without intermission, a public meeting was held every evening, the church being frequently unable to hold them all; while at my own house at ten o'clock in the forenoon crowds assembled in deep spiritual anxiety. For some days every room in my house had a 'stricken' soul in it, surrounded by a small group of praying friends, no bustle or no noise being allowed, but all calm, solemn, prayerful, reading God's Word, or singing a psalm, as the case might require. After some eight days the 'striking down' and all external manifestations nearly ceased, except a case at intervals; but there appeared no abatement of religious concern or cessation of the Spirit's influence. Whole households were awakened and brought to seek the Saviour, and have all ever since 'brought forth fruits meet for repentance.' *Everybody* for a number of weeks was moved, and all seemed to think they should seek salvation, feeling as if they were on the very verge of the spiritual and the eternal world, and in the immediate presence of Diety. There has been an 'abounding in prayer,' and an insatiable thirst for the Word of God."

About the middle of June the revival wave swept on to Saintfield. There had for some time previously been an unusual earnestness and desire after Divine things on the part of many of the people.

The Sabbath before the movement began was a solemn day. At the close of his sermon Mr Mecredy, addressing his people, observed that he had now been among them for eleven years, and though he had laboured earnestly for their salvation, he could not lay his hand on one to whom he could refer as savingly impressed through his instrumentality. He then entreated that prayer should be offered by those who knew and prized the privilege for the outpouring of the Spirit on the place. A few evenings after, at a united meeting, held in conjunction with the Rev. Samuel Hamilton, the minister of the first Presbyterian church, in which there has been an extensive awakening, the gracious influence began to descend which so abundantly refreshed the weary heritage.

Night after night, as elsewhere, the people flocked in crowds together, and multitudes were deeply affected and impressed. The joy of the converted knew no bounds; they burned with intense desire for the conversion of all around, and could with difficulty be induced to take their necessary sleep.

It were easy to multiply cases, but it is enough to know that a great and cheering work has been going forward in all that neighbourhood. With some, impressions that were only transient and the effect of temporary excitement, are dying away; and others, who were for the time outwardly reformed, are falling again into their old sins. But the life and reality of religion have been brought home to many as they never were before. The dead have been awakened, and those who were ready to die have been raised up to newness of life.

A short stage by rail onward is Ballinahinch. The

ministers here also waited long, as they imagined, before they witnessed any decided indications of a gracious work in their own bounds. In the calm of a summer evening, however, whilst one of them was addressing a number of persons in the open air, and recommending an organisation of prayer-meetings in the district, the audience were all at once arrested by a piercing cry, which invested the scene with a new interest; and though many months have since elapsed, the influence of that meeting is distinctly felt by many to this hour. It is unnecessary to enter into details. Enough to say that every testimony of the Divine presence, elsewhere vouchsafed, was experienced at Ballinahinch. Prayer-meetings sprang into existence, and helpers were raised up on every side. The work was full of labour, but it was also full of life and joy. It was the season when visitors, in large numbers, frequent the place to drink the waters, and many of these entered with the deepest interest into the movement, and contributed their best assistance.

Of the many gratifying results, one has been the establishment of a free school in the week evenings, in which, under a goodly band of devoted teachers, no less than a hundred and twenty adults are trained in ordinary as well as in religious knowledge.

The following striking incident, one of many, is mentioned by the Rev. S. J. Hanson, late of Conlig, now of Kingstown. It is here recorded as an *encouragement to prayer* :—

"I had gone to Coleraine to witness the movement there ; and, having ascertained that that place, so richly watered by the outpouring of the Spirit, had been made the subject of special prayer by the Ahoghill converts, I resolved to request the prayers of those lately awakened on behalf of Conlig. On the following week I was in Comber, addressing a meeting for Mr Rogers, and during my address my resolution flashed over my mind. I seized the suggestion, and then and there besought God's children to join in prayer for Conlig. I returned home the following day, and found, on arriving, that there had been a messenger for me. I immediately set out for the place from which the messenger came, and, to my delight, there found a soul rejoicing in Jesus. On making inquiry as to the time and circumstances of the merciful visitation I learned that, at the very time Mr Rogers's people were engaged in prayer for us, this woman awoke from sleep, repeating Isaiah lii. 2, ' Shake thyself from the dust ; arise and sit down, O Jerusalem ; loose thyself from the bands of thy neck, O captive daughter of Zion.' Such was the introduction of the revival work here, as if, in answer to special prayer, God was encouraging us to climb more frequently the Mount of Intercession by this token of assurance that the prayer of the righteous availeth much."

Within a short distance of Donaghadee, on the sea-coast, is a rural district called Ballycopeland. The Rev. Robert Black thus records the commencement of the awakening in that neighbourhood :—

" When the revival visited Millisle the whole village was moved. Few retired to rest, crowds collected around the doors of the awakened ones to hear them cry for mercy—such a night was never witnessed here. This greatly intensified the feeling.

" From that date there was no difficulty in collecting a large meeting on any day of the week, with the shortest notice. I may say that *open-air* services were held here throughout the entire summer, on the Sabbath evenings, with an attendance varying from three hundred to twelve hundred of all classes in the district—high and low, rich and poor, moral and immoral—listening, not only with attention but with deep earnestness, to plain gospel truths proclaimed in the name of Christ.

" There have been many cases of revival, properly so called—*i.e.* Christians quickened to newness of spiritual life. I will just notice one case. James —— is a quiet, unobtrusive man, about sixty years old, of that rank in life which depends on daily labour for support. He has been, I believe, in Christ ever since I have known him. One night his mind was so engaged with religious thought that he could not sleep. He rose and prayed almost the entire night. His mind was similarly engaged for many nights."

Among those engaged during the summer of 1859 in the advancement of the work of God, were many young men in course of preparation for the ministry. A goodly number of these were themselves quickened into newness of life, and willingly consecrated their energies to the holy cause. To such an extent were they thus employed, that when the period arrived for the bestowal of the degrees and other literary and scientific honours, annually awarded by Queen's University, several of the undergraduates were found to have withdrawn for the time from the competition—a circumstance which was publicly noticed at the time, both by the Vice-Chancellor of the University and by his Excellency the Lord-Lieutenant of Ireland. The theological students were especially serviceable in their respective neighbourhoods, and the experience they acquired within the few months referred to, gave them a profounder insight into the mode of

THE REVIVAL IN COUNTY DOWN

dealing with individual souls than they could have attained by whole years of academic training.

I have much gratification in introducing here a statement by one of the young men who were actively occupied in the work. Mr James Heron thus describes the movement in Rathfriland, his native place:—

"Though the late remarkable awakening burst forth suddenly upon the people of Rathfriland and its neighbourhood, yet it did not come unsought for; it came not without many an earnest wish and many a fervent prayer.

"Its presence was first manifested on Saturday evening the 9th of July 1859. Only a few persons, however, were 'stricken' on the occasion; but enough to excite the curiosity and wonder of the whole neighbourhood. It was announced that the young man whose address had been attended with such singular results, would appear before the union prayer-meeting on Sabbath evening. I should have observed that the young man in question had been affected in Belfast, under the address of a Ballymena convert, and had come to relate his experience, and to testify in behalf of the cause of Christ, to the people of Rathfriland. The news of the Saturday-evening's meeting had already spread far over the country. Hundreds who had come from a distance remained for the evening services, and crowds flocked from every direction, expecting to hear and to see wonders. So great was the multitude, that it was soon found necessary to retire to a field in the vicinity of the town. The exercises of praise and prayer were conducted by one of the ministers. The youthful speaker then rose, and proceeded to address the vast assemblage with the utmost coolness. The discourse had not continued fifteen minutes when the audience began to be stirred. A venerable-looking old man sank to the ground close by the platform. Apparently he had swooned, and he was removed out of the crowd as speedily as possible. The silence of the multitude became breathless; the feelings were deeply intense. But the solemn stillness was soon broken by a faint cry which was raised on the opposite side of the platform to that where I had taken my stand. I had scarcely time to turn myself, when, sudden as a gunshot, a strong woman sent forth an unearthly scream at my very side. In a moment she was upon her knees, crying, as she clapped and wrung her hands alternately in wild excitement, 'Oh! my heart. Oh! my hard heart.' The crowd was convulsed, and shook like aspens in the breeze. The voice of the speaker was soon drowned amid the shrieks; the air was filled with groans and screams for mercy. Crowds gathered and pressed around to listen to the lamentations, and here and there to the fervent appeals of the awakened. It was not till long after nightfall that a large portion of the helpless mourners were carried to their homes.

"A tremendous awakening had taken place. During the week that followed, the meetings were continued, and the prostrations did not in the least subside. It seemed, indeed, as if a new era had dawned. Men and women left their ordinary avocations to talk about their souls and the strange sights they had witnessed. The public mind was pervaded with awful solemnity, and that whole week seemed a protracted Sabbath.

"Languishing Christians have been stirred up to vigorous activity, and mere professors have been seriously alarmed. Nowhere, however, has such a change been wrought as upon those whose lives were openly immoral, or who entertained an utter disregard to the observance of religious duties. Considering the very low ebb to

THE REVIVAL IN COUNTY DOWN

which true religion had declined, and, in many cases, the looseness of moral principle, before this great awakening passed over the land, and comparing this with the state of religion and morality which now prevails, one cannot but be amazed at the magnitude of the change that has taken place. Drunkards have been reformed into sober men, Sabbath-breakers have been led to respect the Sabbath, profane swearers have ceased to blaspheme; old injuries have been forgiven, private animosities forgotten, by parties long at enmity. Families in which God was never worshipped, where the Word of God was seldom, if ever, read, where the name of Jesus was only mentioned to be blasphemed, have now the family altar raised in the domestic circle, make the Scriptures their daily study and delight, and reverence and love the sweet name of Jesus beyond every name. Prayer especially, which used to be a wearisome duty to those who still clung to religious forms, has become a pleasant exercise, accompanied with stronger faith and deeper fervency; and every one now reads his Bible. God's Book is made the book of re-reference, and preferred to any other."

The town of Banbridge is one of the most important in the county in which it is situated. For the last few years an unwonted interest in religion has been created in the young men of the locality, mainly through the devoted labours of a Christian layman residing there. As the result of his exertions, the most important moral and spiritual changes had been going forward, and the way seemed to be prepared for a still more extensive spiritual visitation.

The following brief statement of the origin and character of the awakening in Banbridge is interesting, not only for the facts it contains, but as being contributed by a devoted layman of the Episcopal Church, who, during a twelve years' residence in Spain, in the capacity of a civil engineer, applied himself, while constructing some of the leading railroads in that country, no less assiduously to the preparation of that "way of the Lord" along which the gospel chariot has even already commenced its onward progress in that land.

"I returned from Spain," says my esteemed corrrespondent, Wm. Greene, Esq., "towards the close of 1858. In the month of December I was invited to Banbridge by a Christian friend, to a meeting of the Young Men's Association. We numbered about forty on that occasion. Several of us spoke, and many earnest prayers that the Lord would pour out His Spirit on that place were offered. The Lord was among us that evening, and we all seemed to feel His presence in no common way. Towards the close of the proceedings I felt impelled to say that I was certain He was about to do a great work in that town. This was fully six months before the revival was experienced in this country.

"Prayer-meetings were held from time to time, and month after month passed, but no sign was given. At length I was present at a solemn meeting. I could not refrain from tears at the earnest spirit evinced by all. We parted, however, without having witnessed anything uncommon but intense earnestness. It was about three days afterwards, when the same persons were assembled, that the blessed showers came down to refresh the waiting hearts of God's people. Such sights as were witnessed on that night it would not be possible to describe. Multitudes had their stony hearts broken under the subduing influences of the Divine Spirit.

"Soon after I was in the neighbourhood again, and

went in the evening with the same friend to a prayer-meeting. On our way, about half-a-mile from the town, we went into two lowly dwellings ; and in a few minutes there gathered around us eight or nine, who seemed to be filled with joy and peace. We remained but a short time to pray and exhort, and then went off. Scarcely had we got to the door of the Presbyterian church, which was very full, when we met some sin-sick ones being carried, one after another, to the school-house adjacent, crying and sobbing in indescribable agony. Some received peace in answer to earnest prayer whilst there, and many were taken to their own homes. I think it was on that night that a woman of the town, who had been pursuing her sinful course, standing on the bridge enticing the passers-by as they came from the meeting, was shot by an arrow from the unerring bow. She was carried to her house—I was going to say her home. But what a home ! Her bed of straw was on the cold ground. I visited her with my friend a day or two after. But the house of 'ill-fame' was now a house of prayer, and never shall I forget the lowliness of that poor pardoned soul as she prayed by her bed of straw. This case attracted the attention of several persons of similar condition in the same street ; and I have heard since that as many as twenty had given up their evil courses, although some have fallen away since.

" A good man, hearing the story of the 'unfortunate' above mentioned, immediately opened his house to her, and from that time to this has supplied all her wants. Such acts as this are worthy to be chronicled for the benefit of future generations."

The following account of the revival in the parish of

Dromara has been supplied by the Rev. W. J. Patton, minister of the Second Presbyterian Church there:—

"On the 25th of July about a thousand persons assembled in Mr Craig's church for prayer. A deep solemnity pervaded the meeting. Many sobs were heard, many tears were shed, and many were the 'groanings that could not be uttered.' The meeting closed, and all separated for their homes. Shortly afterwards intelligence arrived that some persons had been 'stricken' on their way home. We started off, and the scene which met our gaze will not soon be forgotten. There, on the roadside, with their backs against the ditch, and their faces toward heaven, lay seven persons, supplicating mercy. They were all young and unlearned, yet so scriptural and appropriate were their prayers, that to me and to the large concourse who listened they seemed to be suggested by Him who has been promised to 'help our infirmities.'

"A young girl was heard to assign as a reason why she had not attended the meeting just described, that she was afraid of being seized, and thus rendered unable to be present at the wedding of a friend, to which she had been invited. The marriage morn arrived, and the ceremony was performed. At the suggestion of some of the party, the feasting and the mirth gave place to praise and prayer, and this girl and her sister bridesmaid began to sob and weep, and, in accents which cannot be described, to call for mercy in the name of Jesus. Since that time she has given every evidence of being espoused to Christ. Truly the prayer of faith was heard. The Lord and His disciples were bidden guests. The same Jesus who graced the marriage in Cana did not deny His presence to the humble villagers of Dromara.

"On the evening following this—the 29th July—a

THE REVIVAL IN COUNTY DOWN 137

prayer-meeting was held on the green beside my church, that building being unable to contain the two thousand or more who were present; and at the same place on the succeeding Sabbath evening there was another meeting, attended by not fewer than three thousand. Those were two evenings long to be remembered. On the first not fewer than fifty persons, and on the second about seventy, young and old, men and women, stretched on the green sward, were heard openly to bewail their sins before God, and ask forgiveness in the name of Jesus. In some few this was accompanied with strange convulsions of body; but in most of those affected there was nothing but tears and groans and earnest prayers. One young girl remained seven hours on her knees. Another resolved that she would neither eat nor drink till she had found Christ. I went into the church and looked around. Many were there attending their friends. But others also had come in. In one seat were three girls kneeling in prayer; in another were two others; in another still, were two boys, and so throughout the house. Coming out, I looked into the session-room, and there were five or six boys, belonging to my Bible class, upon their knees. One was praying—' Lord Jesus, pardon my sins; they are so great that crimson and scarlet are no name for them '—and yet there was not a better behaved boy in all the country. They continued there for some hours offering prayer in turn.

" I shall briefly mention a few of the changes which the revival has produced in the parish. Formerly the Bible was little read—now there are few families in which it is not read each day. Formerly many did not pray in private, or if they did, it was only as a matter of form. Now, I believe, there are few who do not, morning and evening at least, and many more frequently, bow their knees to the God of all grace. And, oh, how earnest they are to be kept from sin ! How many earnest, beautiful prayers I have heard of late ; and how many have ascended up on high !

" Formerly not five out of a hundred observed family worship—now, I should say, two-thirds of the people do so. In many a house the son or daughter leads the family devotions, when the father is unable or unwilling."

13

The Revival in the City and County of Derry

I CANNOT better introduce the notice of the work in Derry than by inserting a letter with which I have been favoured from the Rev. Robert Wallace, a highly-esteemed minister of the Wesleyan body, then in that city. His relation to the Church of which he is a minister enables him to testify to the work, not in Derry only, but in other districts :—

" Very early in the year my attention was directed to some remarkable accounts of what was said to be a great revival, accompanied by extraordinary manifestations. On comparing these with what I had read of revivals in England, Scotland, and America, I soon came to the conclusion that it was a work of God, and with others began to look for the gracious visitation in the city of Derry, where I was placed at the time. More than three months passed away, however, before we had anything more than a general spirit of expectation. Early in the summer, arrangements were made to invite from Ballymena and Ballymoney a number of those who had been recently brought under gracious influence, and it was agreed that they should take a part in the public services in the Presbyterian and Wesleyan churches, and also in the open air at the market-place. At these services great crowds attended. The persons recently awakened spoke with great simplicity of the wonderful change that God had wrought in them by grace in the course of the last few weeks or days. A solemn awe rested upon the people; several were stricken down in the manner we had heard of, and a still greater number were cut to the heart, and earnestly sought the Lord. At the commencement of the meetings a number of ministers, representing various denominations, met at the house of the senior Presbyterian minister, and arranged plans for combined efforts to promote the cause of God; and in this manner a service was held in the market-place every evening throughout the summer. The utmost unity prevailed, and this greatly tended to deepen the interest among the people.

"The prominent features of the revival, so far as came under my notice, were—the suddenness of the awakening, the bodily prostrations, and the great extent to which the whole people were impressed. The peculiar features were—that, unlike any formal revival, it had the countenance of almost the entire secular press; that it was not confined to any one denomination, but embraced all Evangelical Churches; and that up till the present time all these have maintained an unprecedented unity. I consider it the most glorious work of God ever known in this country in so short a time; and although we have not the excitement of last summer and autumn, I believe there is a religious influence upon the people of Ulster surpassing anything ever before realised."

In continuation of the narrative of the work in Derry, the Rev. Richard Smyth observes:—

"At a morning service, conducted by Mr Smyth of Armagh, a Roman Catholic in attendance had been brought under conviction, and the first person in the evening who was 'stricken' was also a Roman Catholic. When the unearthly cries were uttered, and the name of Jesus sounded over that dense congregation from the lips of a sinner who felt herself on the brink of hell, a thrill passed through every heart that is utterly indescribable. The whole auditory seemed smitten with a sudden and universal paralysis. They went home, but many were ill at ease. Religion had assumed a new aspect; there appeared to be in it work for the heart of man, and multitudes felt that hitherto they had misunderstood its nature. Some have told me that they never closed an eye that night, but the 'visions of their head troubled them on their beds.' They rose and dragged themselves to their business with the arrow of God fast in their souls, or sat in their rooms communing with distressed hearts. Next evening a meeting was held in the same church, addressed by a number of ministers, in calm and unimpassioned terms; and at that meeting there could not have been less than fifty savingly impressed. Not more than ten suffered from physical prostration, and these cases did not assume any cataleptic type. The work had graciously begun, and an earnest had been given of the showers of blessings that have descended since.

"We have had in this city comparatively few cases of bodily affection or prostration—not one in ten—perhaps not one in twenty. One of the most trying and really distressing cases that came under my observation was that of a girl who imagined herself in hell for three hours, and still out of the depths of hell cried to Jesus for mercy. Her face during this time gave one the idea of a lost soul; there was over it the shadow of a hopeless immortality. At the end of three hours she fell into a kind of trance. Her face resumed its natural appearance; it then became unnatural once more, but in a different manner, the radiance of glory overspread it, and for four hours she seemed to be in the regions of the blest. Of the 'visions' she had during that time she never wished to speak, and I never encouraged her to do so, for I knew her mind to have been strung to an ecstatic pitch; but I rejoice to say that she continues steadfast in the faith of Jesus, and is an example of humility and love, and all the other graces of the Spirit. I have much delight in testifying that I am not aware of one single 'stricken' case in Derry that has turned out to be spurious.

Agencies Employed.—" Except at the first two meetings, we dispensed entirely in Derry with the aid of converts in addressing meetings. Those who were brought to Jesus in the revival were of incalculable aid at anxious inquirers' meetings, in praying with the convinced and distressed, in conversing with the anxious, in directing the perplexed, and in visiting from house to house; but they never took part in the public meetings in the city. Many of the young men in the city were, indeed, much blessed in other districts of the country—in Donegal, Tyrone, Fermanagh, and Cavan. Some of them speak with much power and fervour, and I can testify (for I took some of them with me to meetings in the country) that their simple and heart-stirring words were acknowledged of God to the rousing of many a careless sinner.

Extent of the Work.—" I am not acquainted with any locality where the gracious work was more general among all classes of the community than here. There was an impression abroad, especially at a distance from the revival districts, that it was only the ignorant and those in the humbler ranks of life who were visited with the influence of the revival. I believe that impression to have been unfounded regarding every locality, and most certainly regarding Derry. From the highest to the lowest, not only were serious impressions predominant but the evidences of saving conversion were afforded.

REVIVAL IN CITY AND COUNTY OF DERRY 143

Men of education, men of business talents, and women of refined mental culture were brought to weep and lament over their unbelieving hearts, and had eventually their sorrow turned into joy.

"On the other hand, the Spirit of God reached the most illiterate, and in many instances, where not a letter of the alphabet was known, the name of Jesus and His redemption were familiar to the heart and lip.

"All denominations in the city partook of the gracious shower; the zeal of believers was quickened; and if the revival had done nothing else save stirring up God's people to greater and more combined efforts for the extension of Messiah's kingdom, it would have been no mean result of the holy and grand excitements of the year 1859. I am not prepared to endorse all that has been said about the actual number of conversions, for I have seen statements put forward that conversions in this city are to be numbered by thousands. That I do not believe; and nothing is to be gained by exaggeration. At the last communion in the First Presbyterian Congregation in the city there were about one hundred communicants above the average, and when I remember that there were perhaps not much less than a hundred Sabbath-scholars savingly impressed who did not come to the Lord's table, I am free to give my opinion that in that congregation there were perhaps two hundred brought into the fold of Jesus. Take this, along with the revival of God's own saints, and you form some conception of what God has done for us. But this is what has been done in all the congregations in the city in, I should say, like proportion, some more and some less.

Cases of Conversion.—" A young man of loose habits was walking up the wall of Derry one night about midnight, and seeing a light in a church he walked in to see what was going on. He observed in the church groups of persons here and there, and one of these specially attracted his attention, where about twenty individuals were gathered round a double pew. He marched up the aisle to this group, and with indifferent air took up his place among them. A boy had been 'stricken' in the pew (son of a most worthy and respectable sea-captain), and some nine or ten boys were on their knees around him, alternately praying for the peace of the distressed boy's soul. Our profligate visitor looked on and listened. The scene was new, and he began to feel his knees smiting against each other. At last the stricken boy began to pour out his soul in strains of the most exalted prayer, and then it resolved itself into thanksgiving and praise. This being over, the boy prayed for unconverted people in the city of Derry, and wrestled with God, like Jacob besidet he brook. There was one soul in the surrounding group that was bending like a forest tree. Each word, as it rose from the lips of the ecstatic boy, fell on the soul of that other like a coal of fire. At last he gave way, fell down, and cried most piteously for mercy. Those terrible moanings are in my ears to this hour. He arose in a few minutes, but fell down again like one paralysed. He leaned his head on a form, and the tears streamed to the floor. A young man came forward—one who had himself been brought to Jesus a year ago—and not knowing who the young man was, lifted up his head to see the weeping face, and tears of joy sprung from his eyes as he exclaimed, 'It's my brother George!' Next day he had laid hold of the hope set before him, and he has since given all credible tokens of being a 'new creature in Christ Jesus.'

"Time would fail me to describe other marvels of Divine sovereignty in the conversion of souls. I know well one most interesting family, where a father, an aged man, and six grown-up children have all been brought to Jesus, and are rejoicing in the hope of the glory of God.

General Results.—" The first and most valuable result is the delightful spirit of Christian union. In speaking of Christian union in Derry, I grieve to be obliged to ignore the Episcopal element in its clerical phases. The clergy would not unite with ' Dissenters.' though the people have in general exhibited a most conciliatory and charitable spirit. It is but fair to say that the Episcopal laity at first showed every disposition to unite in prayer-meetings until their leaders endeavoured to infuse into them another spirit. The rest of the community are one. We know one another better, and appreciate each other more. There is now that interchange of genuine feeling which is the characteristic of true spirituality. ' Each one accounts the other better than himself.' "

Among the congregations first visited in County Derry by the revival was that of Maghera, of which an account is given as follows by the Rev. Thomas Witherow :—

" On Thursday, the 2nd of June 1859, the first indications of the presence of the revival appeared at Maghera. On that day a young man, called Thomas Campbell, came over from County Antrim to see his friends at Culnady—a village two miles from this town, on the way to Portglenone, and, while describing at the fireside to his relatives and neighbours the strange scenes which for some time past he had witnessed at religious meetings held beyond the Bann, suddenly the servant-boy in the family was affected with all the usual symptoms. While those present gathered round him in astonishment and alarm, the servant-girl was affected ; and soon afterwards, the brother of the speaker, George

Campbell, a young lad of some seventeen years of age. The prostrations that occurred on this occasion could not have arisen from excitement. It was understood that, up to the evening in question, none of these persons had been under religious concern; no attempt had been made in the neighbourhood to produce a revival; public attention had not been drawn to the subject further than by a narrative of the work going on at Connor and Ahoghill, given from the pulpit on the previous Monday by Rev. Jonathan Simpson, which it is not probable any of the parties referred to had been present to hear. The place where they were struck down was the fireside of a farm house, when they were listening to the conversation of the friend who, in the district of the County where he lived, had witnessed prostrations, but had never been prostrated himself. There was no exposition of Divine truth, no appeal to the passions, no excitement beyond what the novel and interesting incidents related might be supposed to produce. Word of what had occurred soon spread through the village, neighbours gathered in, and the whole night was spent in prayer and in singing praises to God.

"Early in the morning a message was despatched for me, and about ten o'clock I reached the spot in company with a friend. Groups of people, with anxiety and terror pictured on their faces, were collected on the streets of the village, waiting our arrival, and discussing among themselves, in subdued tones, the strange things that had occurred. The first case which we saw was a poor woman, the mother of a number of young children, who had that morning gone to visit those who had been stricken on the previous night, and who had instantly been affected herself. She was an ignorant woman of her class, who had been living an irreligious life, and had not been in the habit of attending any place of worship. We found her stretched upon the bed in her little cabin in a state of great physical weakness, but talking incessantly about her sinful life, and about Satan, 'that beast,' as she called him, who sought her destruction, and about Christ, who had saved her from ruin. She talked in a wild incoherent way, reminding the bystanders of one who was 'drunk with new wine,' and quoted so many texts of Scripture as surprised us all, who knew she could not read, and had not the advantage of public instruction for many years. The servant-girl who had been affected the previous night was found by us apparently exhausted, but in a quiet state, and not seemingly disposed to communicate her feelings. On seeing me enter she lifted her head from the pillow of the bed on which she had stretched herself, and said, 'O Sir, God has been with us this morning.' The servant-man did not say much, but gave us to understand that the burden of sin, which he said was pressing his heart, was not yet removed. It was different with George Campbell, the young lad previously mentioned. He had enjoyed the advantages of better instruction in the Scriptures than any of the others, and now the previous knowledge he had acquired became available. We found him sitting on his bed, surrounded by the neighbours who had gathered in, and singing the 20th Psalm with a heart and spirit such as I have seldom heard thrown into a song of praise. After prayer, he exhorted the friends who had crowded in, telling them how God had delivered him from his sins, and made him a partaker of His grace. 'Oh,' said he, in the most earnest and impassioned manner, 'there was a mountain of sin pressing on my heart, but God in mercy sent the arrows of His love, and pierced that mountain through and through, and it is gone.' Then he warned all against sin, especially the sin of drunkenness, denouncing the public-house as 'the broad road to hell'; and, striking with great violence the Bible which he held in his hand, he shouted, 'Who would dare to ask me to enter a public-house now?' He called on all present to renounce their sins else they would be lost, and spoke to them of Christ with a pathos and energy that drew tears from many eyes. This address, coming from a young lad who one day before would not have ventured to open his lips to any human being on the subject of religion, evidently made a deep impression. The news of these things spread over the whole district in a single day. As my friend and I returned home in the afternoon, the people in the fields threw down their implements of labour, and ran to the wayside to speak to us as we passed; and to each party in succession we had to stop and tell the wonderful things we had seen and heard. This was the origin of the movement at Maghera.

"So soon as a sufficient number of young men had been awakened and converted they immediately showed an inclination to be active and useful. Prayer-meetings were established in town and country; Sabbath-schools which had been suspended were revived; and at the various meetings held in the town and country, the young men attend, and either lead in prayer or deliver addresses, as their capacity enables them. One of these meetings has been held *every morning* for the last six months, and is conducted by the young men of the town; another, attended exclusively by females, is held every Friday evening, at which some twelve or thirteen of the young ladies of the congregation officiate each in her turn. Every country district also has its prayer-meeting. In general they are all well attended, and have done much good.

"The results so far have been very beneficial. The popular feeling is much more favourable to religion. Attendance on the means of grace has been improved. Nineteen pounds' worth of Bibles and Testaments were sold during 1859 at our village depository, whereas the average of other years was no more than six. Domestic prayer has been commenced in many families where it was formerly neglected, the young of both sexes in many instances discharging the duty that is generally expected from the father; while drunkenness and immorality are neither so public nor so prevalent as in former times."

"We also," says the Rev. James Wilson of Lecumpher, "have had most wonderful and impressive scenes, all indicating the sovereignty and gracious character of the work. We have had convictions, not only in the church but in the family, in the absence of all excitement, and not a few during the silence of the night season. So far as I have seen, they have been attended with good."

In the town of Limavady, the movement commenced toward the end of the month of May in pretty much the usual manner. In a short time the entire vale of the Roe was the scene of most intense emotion. Business was all but suspended. Nothing was thought or talked of in every circle but the wonders incomprehensible on every hand around. "A thrill of solemn dread," says the Rev. N. M'A. Brown, " passed like an electric current, from the one end of the Presbytery to the other. The twelve congregations were all assembled in crowded houses in the course of a few days, and multitudes in each were crying for mercy in screams of agony.

"From Sabbath the 12th June till the present time a united meeting of all the Presbyterian congregations in town has been held daily ; multitudes of converts, young and old, being most ready to engage in religious exercises.

" A wonderful impetus was given to the good work by the frequent visits and addresses of friends from Scotland and elsewhere, but especially of Mr Guinness and Brownlow North, Esq. The former addressed some three thousand persons in the open air with effect and acceptance ; but the impression produced by Mr North was deeper still, and doubtless will be more lasting."

In a conversation with Mr Brown, since the above was written, I learned the gratifying fact that, as one of the happy results of the movement, no less than eight young men, of whom six have almost arrived at maturity, were led to commence the work of preparation for the Christian ministry. They are all now regularly applying themselves with this view to their studies, while, at the same time, they lend their assistance, as they have opportunity, to the conducting of the religious exercises in connection with the daily meeting for prayer.

The Rev. Thomas Y. Killen, of Ballykelly, after narrating the mode in which the work began among the people of his charge, thus proceeds to describe its progress and results :—

The Converts—Their Addresses and Prayers.—" For some time at first, some of those who had been converted during the revival addressed the meetings,— relating their own experience—telling how it was with them in the days of their unregeneracy —how they had tasted the pleasures of sin and the world, and found them vain and unsatisfying—how they had been awakened to a sense of their guilt and danger, and led to see the refuges of lies in which they had hitherto trusted—and how the Spirit of God had revealed Christ to their souls as the only Saviour for guilty sinners. These addresses were generally simple, scriptural, and earnest—sometimes most touching and beautiful; and coming, as they did, from the lips of young persons well known to those present, and who, they were all aware, would have previously shrunk from opening their lips in the presence of others, produced a profound impression. Always at the close of their statements they prayed; and if absorbing fervency, and childlike confidence, and deep self-abasement, and powerful pleading constitute the very essence of prayer, then I have indeed listened during the past summer to some of the most genuine specimens of true prayer it has ever been my lot to hear. Very few of the converts were willing to address our congregational meeting after the first statement of their experience. Many of them, however, are still ready to lead in prayer, and take their part in conducting district meetings.

" Besides the prayer-meetings now in operation, which are conducted by adults, a number of the children of one of our daily schools remain by themselves twice a week, after school hours, for mutual prayer. The meeting was commenced of the free motion of the children, and without the knowledge of the teacher.

Preaching and its Effect.—" Formerly it was almost impossible to make one's hearers *feel* under the preaching of the Word. While the revival prevailed in its intensity, preaching was doubtless easier and pleasanter work than ever before, for the simplest truths, presented in the plainest form, were greedily drunk in by the hearers; but, in another sense, more difficult, for there was such tenderness of conscience on the part of the young Christians, that one could scarcely address a word of warning to the impenitent, or point out the works of sinners in Zion, without exciting in their minds the fear that they were, after all, deceiving themselves, and plunging them into the depths of despair.

"At the dispensation of the Lord's Supper there were deep and solemn feelings, more so than I ever witnessed here, and I believe God's children felt that they were seasons of special and real fellowship with Jesus. When the session met for the final examination of the candidates on their knowledge and Christian experience, one of the elders, seeing among them a child of twelve years, said, 'I have great doubts about the propriety of admitting any so young.' 'Well,' said I, 'we must wait till we have examined them, and judge of them individually by their answers.' One after another appeared before us, till it was the turn of that little girl; and when she had replied to the usual doctrinal and experimental questions, it was an impressive sight to see the tears trickling from the eyes of the elders; while the one who made the above remark stood up, and, with deep emotion, declared that now he could say nothing against it. We have agreed to observe the Lord's Supper quarterly for the time to come, instead of half-yearly as heretofore.

The Prostrations.—" For a time we had, both at the ordinary service of the Sabbath and the meetings during the week, a great number of bodily prostrations. They were not produced by crowded meetings—many of them occurred in the open air, in the cool of the summer evenings, some of them in the fields, and some by the roadside, as parties were returning home at midnight, and some in their own houses. There was nothing unusually exciting in the sermons. They commenced here while I was preaching an old sermon, delivered years before to my former charge without producing any visible effect, and to which, from want of time for preparation, I was obliged that day to resort. Indeed, many of the sermons I preached last summer had been delivered elsewhere without exciting any emotion.

"At present we have not by any means the same liveliness which we had some months ago, even among true Christians; and those who only experienced passing convictions are going back to their old sins. Still, I have every reason to believe there has been a most genuine work of grace in many hearts, whose fruits will never pass away; and on conversing with those who have, I trust, been savingly impressed, I find that they continue in a tender frame, and are diligent in the discharge of their personal and social duties."

One of the many places early visited in County Derry was Moneymore, where the work of revival commenced in the beginning of June. The first case was that of one who was a noted drunkard in the neighbourhood, who, as often as he had occasion to visit any of the neighbouring towns, was before he left confined in the "lock-up" for his immoderate use of ardent liquor. After being prostrated several hours he attained true peace, and ever since he has been a new man in his entire habits and character. The manner of his countenance is altogether changed, and it wears an aspect of peculiar sweetness to this day."

The only other incident connected with the work in the same neighbourhood that I shall introduce, is a peculiarly touching one, as follows :—

The Youths' Meeting.—A young lad, aged seventeen, who had been brought to a knowledge of salvation at Coleraine, where he had been in a mercantile establishment, came on a visit to his friends at Moneymore. During the ten days which he spent there, he called together seven others, his young associates, with whom he regularly spent some portion of every day in prayer. The last evening of his visit, they met as usual, and were addressed by him with deep solemnity, when all at once six of the seven fell down imploring mercy. It was not long till they all rose rejoicing, and then, addressing him who alone remained unmoved, they appealed to him and said, " And are you the only one among us who will put Christ to shame ? " when, overcome by their fervent expostulation, he also cried out in the same manner as the rest had done for mercy. Of these seven youths, five are Presbyterians, and have since joined the communion of the Church. The other two are Episcopalians, and, I believe, have also witnessed a good confession. All are reported as consistent in their deportment, and he who was the instrument in drawing them to the possession of like precious faith, has the joy unspeakable of regarding them as given to his entreaties and his prayers.

14

The Revival in County Tyrone

NOT far from Moneymore is the village of Orritor, of which, in connection with the revival, there is one notable incident which may not be omitted here. It may be properly entitled

The Revival in the Fair.—In the beginning of the month of June, there is an annual fair at Orritor. It is a kind of Donnybrook in miniature, and has ever been regarded by the well-disposed as a grievous nuisance, injurious alike to morals and religion. Thither the idle and the profane have been in the habit of resorting from year to year, and there they met with those attractions which best accorded with their depraved taste and desire —the show, the licensed drinking-tent, the gaming-table. It was a scene where Satan held high festival, and whence a noxious influence was diffused over the whole neighbourhood. The Rev. W. Wray, the Presbyterian minister of the place, resolved, during the period of the revival, when an unwonted seriousness and awe pervaded the community, to grapple with this established and gigantic evil. He accordingly announced on the Sabbath previous that divine service would be held in the church at a period when he knew the fair would be at its height, and its frequenters would be in the very heyday of their boisterous revelry. About two hundred persons, at the hour appointed, assembled for religious exercises, which were continued in the church till about three o'clock.

By that time some of his brethren from the neighbourhood, whom the worthy pastor had invited to come to his assistance, had arrived. It was then at once resolved to meet the adversary face to face, and on his own ground. The congregation was immediately dismissed, and marching to a field hard by, the ministers in front, they took up a position right in the very camp of the enemy, their numbers having so much increased on the way that when the service was resumed, they were as four to one compared with those who remained on the fair ground in the pursuit of "vanity." The motley congregation thus attracted were held attentive to the word of truth for hours together; and before they separated, some had given way before the higher Power which lighted upon them, and the noise of riot and dissipation was hushed before the agonised and despairing cry for mercy. Many in other years had taken their first step at this country fair on the downward course of ruin; but a far different experience is associated with its last gatherings, for there are those in that neighbourhood who will never cease to think of these as marking a new era in their history, even the period when they forsook the way of sin and folly, and entered on the path of life and immortality."

In the districts adjacent to that last mentioned there has been a great awakening, with corresponding results.

"If," says the Rev. J. P. Wilson, "we take a district four miles round Cookstown, hundreds have been added to the communion of the Church. Family worship has been established where it was never observed before; people come out to the house of God in greater numbers, and listen with more marked attention; district prayer-meetings are multiplied; drunkards have been reformed;

and neighbourhoods have totally changed their character. Drunkenness and blasphemy have greatly diminished; though, as the larger part of the population is Roman Catholic, and therefore disposed to mock at the revival, we need not be surprised to find cases of drunkenness before our magistrates, or to hear the awful oath from some as they return from market."

To the same effect writes the Rev. J. K. Leslie:—

"I am now busily engaged visiting in the country; and the downright reality of the glorious revival is demonstrated in the extraordinary transformation of character I witness in many families, who, from being the most careless, are now ready for every good work. I never enjoyed such real pleasure in any former visitation of my people. Nothing amazes me more than the number of the prayer-meetings that are established everywhere throughout the country. Neither my brethren nor myself have had anything to do with the formation or sustenance of them. All false delicacy and shame are laid aside in matters of religion, and men and boys that could not be induced to pray before others now do so with effect and profit."

"There has, no doubt," says the Rev. John Maxwell of Brigh, "been largely intermingled with the work of God much both of man and the devil's work that was calculated to do great evil; but the fears I at one time cherished on this matter have to a great extent been agreeably disappointed, and I now am strongly impressed with the conviction that permanent spiritual good will be the result. Of the stricken ones, while some have ended in temporary conviction, I fully believe the great majority were either cases of conversion or the *revival* of genuine Christians. Many have received much spiritual profit where no physical manifestation took place, and I am every week learning new instances of this sort. The mind of one individual gave way under intense conviction, but is now perfectly restored. The 'great fear' which was upon the general population is now passing away, but I trust the good work is still progressing. On last Sabbath evening I was privileged to witness a most refreshing scene, at a service I conducted in Lord Castlestuart's private chapel."

From the many incidents and cases supplied from other districts in Tyrone, I can only select the following:—

The Movable Tent.—" In our districts," writes the Rev. J. M'Askie of Colgherney, " where a prayer-meeting has been held since the month of June last, the attendance was so great that no place could be found large enough to contain the numbers of all denominations who flocked to it. They erected a tent, which is movable, and which, with a barn to which it is always attached, holds about four hundred. I have seen five hundred crammed into it on one of the coldest nights during the winter, and standing for three hours listening with the most intense attention to the preaching of the word."

Things Brought to Remembrance.—" I mention," says the same minister, " the case of an amiable young girl, as one of the most striking fulfilments of the promise, ' He shall teach you all things, and brings all things to your remembrance,' it has been my privilege to witness. She was stricken at a meeting in B., with some others. When returning to consciousness, or rather, when recovering the use of speech—for she appeared to be totally unconscious of the presence of any one, as she lay with eyes turned up to heaven, and fixed—for about four hours she continued repeating sermons and other addresses delivered by myself during the previous month. In many instances she repeated whole passages of them *verbatim*. Pausing at intervals, she would exclaim, ' Oh, what have I not heard ! ' and then she would resume the repetition of some striking passages with a fluency and an accuracy that were perfectly astonishing. But what struck me most in her case was the readiness with which memory called up those portions of the Word of God most suitable under her own peculiar circumstances. Not less than one hundred Scripture texts were repeated, and sometimes half a chapter at once, with the greatest accuracy, and all bearing upon her own case. I have had frequent opportunities of conversing with her since, and, what is very strange, many of the passages in the sermons so fluently repeated that night, seem to be quite forgotten, and the portions of Scripture she could not repeat with the same accuracy. E. J—— is one of the happiest of Christians."

At Castlederg there was a great awakening. From the outset, the Wesleyan and Presbyterian ministers co-operated in the movement—especially at the evening meetings, which were held in the open air during the summer months. Having at a subsequent period visited the place, in connection with the opening of a Presbyterian church, I had an opportunity of witnessing a pleasing instance of the harmony existing between the members of these denominations. The church-going habits of the people were so increased by the revival, that, in anticipation of an attendance at the dedication services beyond what the new structure could possibly accommodate, the Wesleyan brethren had made an offer of their chapel, which was also filled on the day in question by a respectable audience, while another minister, who had been provided in the event of such a necessity arising, officiated. Although the population is chiefly agricultural, the amount raised, so far as I can recollect, was about £130.

The revival in this neighbourhood had an unwonted origin, the agents being not the stated ministers or visitors of the usual class from the awakened districts, but *commercial travellers*, whose business had brought them to the village through some of the towns of Derry and Antrim. " All of these persons," says the Rev. John Crockett, " saw and bore witness to the great change wrought in the hearts of those with whom they were brought into contact. Some of them, who had themselves become the subjects of this change, were led to stop in our town over Sabbath, and being of our communion, attending our services on the Lord's-day, and being known to us, an opportunity was given them to speak to the people after service, and thus to relate what they had seen in others, and what they were made to feel in themselves. This practice was pursued for two or three Sabbaths in my own and the neighbouring congregations, and contributed very much to produce deep and serious impressions on one and all of us."

The town of Strabane is one of the most considerable and important in the county to which it belongs. No great excitement took place among its population, although the most salutary effects are observable among them. The narrative which follows therefore may be regarded as a description of the work in a community in which there was an absence of many of those features which usually characterised it. It has been supplied by Mr J. G. Clarke, a licentiate of the Presbyterian Church, who gave his best assistance to the movement :—

"Immediately after authentic reports had reached us of the Lord's work in Derry and Coleraine, a united meeting for prayer was held in the town Hall, which was so crowded on that occasion that many who arrived late were obliged to go away for want of accommodation. About ten days after, an open-air united meeting for prayer was commenced in one of the enclosed market-places of the town. The hour was eight o'clock in the evening, and the exercises continued usually from an hour to an hour and a half; after which an adjourned meeting was held in the Second Presbyterian church, which was close at hand, when those who were desirous of it had an opportunity of joining in devotional exercises for an hour or more, as the occasion required, but in no case was it considered advisable to keep the people to an unseasonable hour. At the conclusion of each service a considerable number of anxious inquirers remained to speak with the ministers present; but as this arrangement was found to be inconvenient, it was abandoned for the more convenient one of morning classes, at suitable hours for inquirers.

"Besides the evening open-air meeting, there was one held every Tuesday, the market-day of Strabane, in the same place, from twelve to one o'clock. This was attended chiefly by the country people, who had come into town to market, but who gladly snatched an hour from the busy day to devote to eternal interests, and it was ascertained that at almost every meeting some had been awakened to anxiety about salvation.

"Except on two occasions near the commencement of the revival, the services of converts were not in requisition. The meetings were in every case presided over by ministers, elders, or other experienced Christian laymen. In conducting them, ministers of different evangelical denominations in and around Strabane—including those of the General Assembly, Reformed Presbyterian body, and Methodist persuasion—heartily concurred. I am sorry to add that, as in most of the other districts of the country and in the city of Derry, I must except the Episcopalian ministers, who have stood entirely aloof here throughout the whole movement, though numbers of their people have taken a deep interest in the revival, and attended the prayer-meetings with great regularity."

The Rev. James Gibson and the Rev. William Russell, the ministers of the Presbyterian Church in Strabane, confirm all the statements made in the preceding communication.

15

The Revival in County Armagh

I SHALL confine the narrative of the work in this county principally to the statements furnished by the ministers in its two principal towns, Armagh and Lurgan, introducing the latter first, as it was first visited.

"A work of preparation for revival," says the Rev. Lowry E. Berkeley, "had been in progress at Lurgan, as elsewhere, for years prior to 1859. Here the Rev. Thomas Millar, publisher of the *Tracts for Ireland*, lived and laboured. The 'healing leaves' had been scattered on every side. Sabbath-schools had done much for the instruction of the young. A goodly number of earnest Christians were here, who continued in prayer and supplication, expecting a blessing; and they were not disappointed.

The First Convert.—"Early in June, Christian people of different denominations in town manifested a desire to come together for prayer, first in the different congregational prayer-meetings, and afterwards in a neutral place, at the dinner hour of the working classes. These meetings were but begun, when a licentiate of our Church was one night raised out of bed to see a young man in a lodging-house, a stranger, who wished to talk with a Presbyterian minister. The people of the house thought he was beside himself. It was a case of true spiritual conviction. Next day he was rejoicing in Jesus and making Him known, by writing letters to his friends and by the work of tract distribution.

First United Meeting.—" The first meeting for united prayer in which any of the Episcopal ministers took part, was held in the Presbyterian church, on the 28th of June. Hitherto these brethren had rather kept aloof, doubting the real character of the movement, but from this period their doubts seemed to vanish. At that meeting one public conviction took place. It turned out a case, as far as man could judge, of real conversion to God. The court in which the individual who was the subject of it dwelt, resounded for many days with the voice of singing and prayer. It had produced a solemnising effect upon the whole neighbourhood, and it became evident that if Satan was working, it was for the overthrow of his own kingdom.

The Work in the Pastor's Absence.—" I left for the Assembly in Dublin on the 4th of July, having made arrangements for the meetings during that week. On Tuesday evening the second meeting for united prayer, in which all denominations were represented, was held. A student of theology addressed it. There were six cases of public conviction. On their way home, and after reaching it, many were brought to their knees. The next day the people were giving way in all directions. No meetings had been announced for that evening, but the young people and others assembled voluntarily, filled both the school-rooms as well as the church, and continued till two or three o'clock in the morning in singing and prayer. On Thursday it was the same. United exercises were almost impossible. In every pew was a prayer-meeting. Some were prostrated under agonising conviction. Others were rejoicing as having found Jesus. As in Israel of old, it was almost impossible to ' discern the noise of the shout of joy from the noise of the weeping of the people.' It is believed that hundreds were impressed during those two nights, and many of them truly converted to God. The labours of the Rev. Matthew Murphy, the licentiate previously referred to, on this occasion and subsequently, were eminently useful and much blessed.

He is Summoned Home.—" From him I heard, whilst attending the sittings of Assembly, of what was going on, I concluded at once that duty called me home. I left on Friday morning, before a telegram arrived conveying the anxious wish of some of my people for my return. They feared that excitement was going too far. They knew the inflammable materials by which we were surrounded. The enemy would speak reproachfully if any occasion should be given. The multitude came together that evening as usual. I had gathered up, as far as possible, the counsels of the brethren as expressed in the conference at the Assembly, and was prepared to act upon them. The people were exhorted and prayed with, and those who had found Christ were advised to ' go home to their friends, and tell them how great things the Lord had done for them, and how he had compassion on them.' With difficulty they were persuaded to disperse, and after the church was closed, many assembled in the school-rooms adjoining, and continued for a time in devotional exercises.

The New Scenes he Witnesses.—" The next evening there was a delightful meeting, composed very largely of those whose hearts God had touched. Some of the converts prayed. After a short service, those anxious about their souls were invited to remain for conversation. Almost all waited. Every pew was again filled with mourning or rejoicing. Those who had found Christ were inviting others to come to Him. I walked about among them for an hour, speaking a word here and there, but specially intent on observing what was passing. It was a scene over which angels must have rejoiced. Such godly sorrow! Such love to Jesus! Such simple gospel-preaching! Such fervent prayers! In one pew I observed a man sitting, apparently under deep conviction, whilst a lad of fifteen or sixteen years of age was standing with outstretched arm preaching to him Jesus! ' You have only to look to Him, and be saved. Is it possible you will not trust in Jesus?' Out of the mouth of babes praise was perfected.

Classes and Meetings.—" From the first I had classes for inquirers and converts, which were greatly needed and much blessed. At the close of every prayer-meeting (and they were held in the church five evenings each week during the months of July and August), persons anxious about their souls were invited to remain, and warning, instruction, and encouragement were given as might be required. Many meetings for prayer, conducted by members of the church, were at the same time held throughout the country. These still continue, to the number of about *twenty* each week. They are well attended, and have helped greatly to confirm the souls of the disciples.

The Country Districts.—" The movement passed from one part of the country round here to another, and in some places, of course, the impression was more marked and manifest than in others. I remember one day in the beginning of harvest driving out to see a person in a rural district. No work was being done in the neighbourhood. The people were gathered in groups on the public roads, literally walking, and leaping, and praising God, or assembled in their houses engaged in exercises of devotion. No manner of labour was being attended to, though the fields were white to the harvest. The concerns of the soul and eternity were occupying exclusive attention."

Through the kindness of the Bishop of Down, I have been favoured with extracts from letters, in reply to late inquiries, addressed to some of his clergy, as to the "present effects" of the revival. The following is from the Rev. Thomas Knox, rector of Lurgan, and is dated 16th April 1860:—

"1st, Congregations, both in church and at cottage lectures, greatly increased. The increase is composed, in a great measure, of young men and women who were formerly indifferent to spiritual matters. 2nd, The communicants nearly doubled, and from the same class of persons. 3rd, Adult classes have sprung up of persons anxious for instruction. 4th, A young men's society, established by the exertions of my curate, the Rev. T. Cosgrove. They assist in district-visitings, and in distributing tracts that we supply them with. I may also add, that a more religious tone pervades the entire neighbourhood. Drunkenness has declined, and we have observed *no case* of relapse in those who had really been affected at the period of the revival. Two or three Roman Catholics who had then joined our congregations, have been with us ever since, and are daily studying Scripture and attending the classes. These are the principal features. We require accommodation for five hundred more, at least, in the church, which I hope will be ready for them in about eighteen months."

The following, also dated 16th April, is from the Rev. Henry Murphy, rector of Magheralin, in the same neighbourhood:—

"It affords me the most sincere pleasure to be able to say that the effect produced among us answers to the 'cause.' There is a hungering and thirsting after the word of God, as is clearly evinced by the full attendance on every means of grace. My church was built to accommodate five hundred; it is full every Sabbath morning (yesterday there were five hundred and thirty-one); and the evening congregation averages three hundred (it used to be forty or fifty). I have two evening services during the week; one in a school-house, which is always crowded—the other in the church, which is attended by a steady congregation of between three and four hundred. Before this religious awakening (about three years ago), I commenced an evening service in the village; but after some time I discontinued it, because I could get no attendance. Now, had I a service every evening in the week, I could command a meeting. Besides all this, morality, in every sense of the word, is the order of the day. The change, indeed, is a mighty one."

Among the earliest incidents of the revival in Armagh, the following is related by the Rev. J. R. M'Alister, respecting a scene of awakening in a daily, and also in a Sabbath school:—

"One morning, a little girl, about eleven years old, entered my daily female school, lifted up her hands and clasped them, saying, 'Oh! I have found Jesus! I have found Jesus!' There was no minister present; there had been no address delivered to children. The words of the child kindled the flame, and in a few minutes a wail of sorrow ascended to heaven that alarmed the inhabitants of the surrounding houses. As I passed along the street, a boy came in breathless haste to me, and said, 'Come, sir, come, the girls in the school are all crying for mercy.' When I entered, some were lying on the floor, some in the arms of the teacher, some in the arms of the monitor, some in the arms of other children ; floods of tears were flowing ; confession of sin was freely made from little broken hearts ; cries for mercy to God ; supplications for Jesus to come and save them ; earnest prayers for the Holy Spirit to come and take the stony heart out of them, and give them a heart of flesh. A similar scene occurred in my Sabbath-school. Many were stricken down in an hour or two. Young persons of both sexes, from twelve to twenty-two years of age, awakened, agonising under conviction of sin ; lifting up their hands to heaven ; fixing their eyes upon Jesus ; confessing their transgressions : one saying—' I am lost ! I am a child of the devil ; for I have told lies, and the devil is the father of lies ' ; another exclaiming—' Ah ! I have mocked Jesus ! ah ! I have mocked Jesus ! ' another—' What a hypocrite I have been ! ' many from time to time praying—' O Lord ! for Jesus' sake have mercy upon me ' ; ' Lord, open the door of my heart and come in ' ; ' O Jesus, wash me in the fountain of Thy blood,' etc., etc. : the ministers and Sabbath-school teachers moving amidst them travailing in birth till Christ should be formed in them ; praying with them ; singing over them, and directing their souls to the great Physician ; others coming, seeing the wondrous work of the Lord, returning to their homes to render themselves up to God."

The Rev. Jackson Smyth has furnished the following narrative of the work as it came under his inspection :—

The First Moved in the Congregation.—" The first moved in this congregation was an interesting young girl, whom I met in the street one day, weeks before there was any public manifestation in the city. I spoke to her, on meeting her, and her eyes filled with tears. ' What is the matter ? ' I said. Her lips quivered, her chest slightly heaved, and the truth flashed upon my mind. Whereupon I added, ' Are you in concern about your soul ? ' ' Yes, sir,' was said with deep feeling. ' I shall visit you in the evening'; and I did. No one in the house knew her state of mind, as she had not made it known. Her sister wondered that I had all at once taken to visit the family every day, when I had never visited in the house before. These visits continued two weeks, when one day I entered, and there was a calm, sweet expression in her face which told of joy within. ' What account have you to give of yourself to-day ! ' ' I am happy in Christ ; and, oh, what happiness ! ' ' The revival has commenced in Armagh,' I mentally exclaimed, and thanked God. Weeks afterwards, on calling one day at the house where this interesting girl lives (it is a business house), I said to her, ' Now that you have tasted that God is gracious, what would you think of holding a prayer-meeting with your companions every night before going to bed ? ' ' We do that, sir,' was the reply. One after another, the young persons in that house were brought to the Lord, till no fewer than *seven* gave clear indication of hopeful conversion. There was not a case of prostration in the house at all.

The Work becomes Public.—" By and by the work became more public, though there had been a falling off in the attendance at our prayer-meetings. There was an impression abroad that God was not going to visit Armagh. One evening, as we assembled for prayer in the church as usual, the pews were almost empty. I made a few remarks in reference to our wonderful position. Like Gideon's fleece, we were dry whilst all around the earth was watered. A brother minister rose, read a chapter, commented very briefly on it, and gave out a psalm. As he sat down, I whispered to him, ' I see

THE REVIVAL IN COUNTY ARMAGH 171

a young man under deep conviction of sin in one of the pews; he will cry out very soon.' When the singing ceased, the wail rose up to heaven—' O Jesus, have mercy on my soul.' Another voice was heard in the gallery, crying loudly for pardon and acceptance with an offended God. The revival '*had come!*' That first young man was a Sabbath-school teacher, but his teaching had been lifeless till then. Now he teaches with all his soul, and he has been blessed to the conversion of many.

Crying for his Sins.—" This first-fruit of a *public* manifestation of the power of God's Spirit, on the following Sabbath evening held a prayer-meeting in a private house, a little distance in the country, where there were two or three cases of 'striking.' Being members of my congregation, I called on Monday to visit them. Two were rejoicing intensely—a girl of about eighteen years of age, and a boy of about twelve. While I sat, a little boy of five years of age came up and leaned against my knee. I thought this a very unusual thing, for, having come recently to the city, I was quite a stranger. Taking up the little fellow on my knees, I said, ' Well, my boy, do you know anything of Jesus ? ' ' Yes.' ' And what do you know about Him ? ' He paused, and then his mother spoke. ' John (the boy's name) was out yesterday evening in the corner of the adjacent field, when Mr H. was holding a prayer-meeting there. We heard bitter crying, and thinking John was hurt, I ran quickly out. He was coming towards the door, screaming piteously. He threw himself down at the side of the wall, and continued to cry very bitterly. In a little, I heard him utter the word " *Jesus.*" No one disturbed him then. When he had cried for a length of time to Jesus to take away his sins, he paused, rose up, wiped his eyes and cheeks hurriedly, and ran up to me (his mother) and kissed me rapturously. Presently he ran out, and entered a house hard by, and asked a little playmate if he would come and " cry for his sins." His companion was indifferent, wondered what it all meant, and stayed where he was. John returned, and commencing to weep, exclaimed, " T. J—— will not come and cry for his sins." '

" Whilst his mother was giving me this narrative of the evening before, the little fellow sat on my knee with a settled calm in his face, which spoke volumes for the truth of Christianity. Desirous of ascertaining the certainty of his conversion, I called on the following week to make inquiry. ' What about John ? ' ' He has been very quiet during the week, giving no trouble in the house as he used to do, but he is very cheerful. He attends the prayer-meetings in the houses around, and is very attentive.' ' Does he pray at home ? ' ' Yes.' ' Is it only the prayer he used to repeat as a matter of form ? ' ' No, he uses words of his own.' By this time all the children in the house had been convinced of sin, with one exception (a Sabbath-school girl). ' Last night,' continued his mother, ' when I was preparing him for bed, he ran away from me, and knelt down and prayed, " O Jesus, come and pardon the sins of father, and mother, and Charlotte." ' That boy has been most consistent in his demeanour ever since, and is no doubt a trophy of grace, one of those of whom is the ' kingdom of heaven.'

Scene in the Retiring-room.—" The good and glorious work went on. One day in the church, when I had terminated the morning devotional exercises, and was about to commence the exposition of my text, a person cried aloud for mercy ; then another, and another, till about a dozen left the church, or were helped to leave. When I left the pulpit, it was to witness a touching sight in the retiring room. There were seven of a family all

THE REVIVAL IN COUNTY ARMAGH 173

kneeling together—the father a godly man, who had been so for many years. Two daughters already Christians, and the other four crying for mercy. The scene became grand and sublime, when one of the boys arose trusting in Christ, and the father embraced him as a new-born babe in Jesus, and then the other immediately afterwards. These boys have been steady Christians ever since. There was another group, consisting of two young girls, one only about nine years of age, kneeling together. The younger had said on entering the Sabbath-school that morning, ' I am just a week old.' She had been converted the Sabbath before. Now she was kneeling, preaching Jesus Christ to the distressed soul of a young Sabbath-school companion. In another part of the room was still another group. Two girls who had been Unitarians, and had come with their parents to the neighbourhood of Armagh, were convinced of sin, and found peace in the Lord. Tears must have gushed forth from the most obdurate to witness the affectionate embrace of those poor girls, now children of God through faith in Christ Jesus. Their subsequent history furnishes a memorable instance of the power of prayer. Their mother had not been regular in attendance on the public means of grace, and there was no family altar ever erected to the Lord in their home. These girls forthwith commenced the blessed exercise of prayer and reading God's Word in the family. They conducted its exercise in turn—one in the morning, the other in the evening. This continued for some time, till at length the mother became interested. She came out to attend a meeting in a country house where I preached. On the following Sabbath she came to church—was forced to cry out—remained in distress for hours—at length departed to her home, where she soon enjoyed repose in Christ, and now is not ashamed to assist her daughters in their humble yet acceptable service of a kind and gracious God, through Jesus Christ our Lord."

The Rev. Wm. Henderson, another of the Armagh ministers, supplies the following incident:—

"The second person I visited after the revival came had been stricken down in her own dwelling. She was not then connected with my congregation, but nominally belonged to the Established Church. For many years, however, she had not attended any religious service, and, with her husband, was reckoned careless and godless. One evening she returned from her day's labour, and while preparing food for the family she fainted, as her husband thought. She continued for half-an-hour in this state; and on becoming sensible she cried out in fearful agony for mercy and forgiveness. Again she relapsed into the faint, and after a similar period had passed as before, she became sensible, and was rejoicing in the Saviour as *her* Saviour. It was the day following that I first saw her, and she was then happy in the Lord. She told me that Jesus had shown her her sins; that He had shown her His love in taking her sins away, but that she was not at liberty to tell all she saw or heard. Previous to this occurrence little was known of the revival in this immediate neighbourhood, and the woman had no opportunity of becoming acquainted with any of its peculiarities, nor had she been spoken to about her soul by any one. I have seen her often since, and witnessed her conduct, and there is much to make me hopeful of her salvation."

In the month of September a great meeting was held in the open air in the neighbourhood of Armagh, at which fully three thousand persons were present. This meeting was addressed, among others, by the Hon. and Rev. Baptist Noel, who made a tour of the greater part of

THE REVIVAL IN COUNTY ARMAGH 175

Ulster about that time. "Considerable emotion," says the Rev. R. Wallace, of Tottenham, who was present, " soon began to evince itself in the meeting, and during the day many (as many as sixteen came under the personal observation of my friend and fellow-traveller) men, women, and children were struck down and forced to cry for mercy; in all there were about thirty such cases on this occasion. I sat on the platform, and had a commanding view of the countenances of the people during the whole of the service. The excitement was at its height during the address of a young convert, as he detailed God's dealings with himself, and earnestly besought all hearing him to flee from the wrath to come and lay hold on eternal life. And what struck me most of all was, not the case of those who were prostrated and forced to cry for mercy, but the case of those who were manifestly struggling to conceal their convictions and to suppress the rising emotions of their hearts. In many cases I saw the big tear roll down the man or woman's cheek; and I saw strong men seeking to conceal their feelings by hiding their faces in their caps and hats, and leaning upon one another, as hardly able to stand before the preacher's words and appeals. And from what I beheld of this sort, and from the general solemnity and seriousness which pervaded that meeting, it is my conviction that the number of persons *struck down* bears no proportion to the number of those who were really smitten in heart, truly convicted of sin, and made to cry out, although silently, ' What must we do to be saved ? ' "

" The speech of Mr Moore, of Ballymena, struck me as particularly calm, discriminating, excellent, and forcible. He faithfully warned the audience against trusting in the mere physical manifestations or effects, and confounding them with conversion."

The following brief statement by the Rev. J. D. Martin, of Tullyallen, may be taken as a specimen of the work in the rural districts of the same county :—

"On Sabbath, the 30th June 1859, the Rev. S. J. Moore, of Ballymena, came to preach the annual sermon on behalf of the Sabbath-school Union in this quarter, at Tullyallen. The services commenced at five o'clock P.M. The audience was large, amounting to several thousands. Strong men trembled ; faces grew pale ; many could scarcely reach home when the services were ended, through weakness and anxiety, and many as they went were disposed to retire to some solitary place to pray. Such was the state of feeling produced on such a multitude in a few minutes. This was surely the powerful work of the Holy Spirit as on the day of Pentecost. That meeting was kept up for several hours, and was addressed by the ministers of the neighbourhood, who were present. Prayer-meetings were appointed during the week, and on the next Friday evening a large number attended. During the services, fifteen or twenty were impressed or stricken, crying aloud for mercy. The work of revival had now come.

"The attention of the community was quite arrested, and the people spoke of little else but the revival. The business of the world was to a great extent laid aside ; religion seemed to take its proper place—the first place ; the salvation of the soul seemed to be the one thing needful, many almost forgot to take their regular food— became pale and weak. Their great anxiety appeared to be, ' What must I do to be saved ? '

"Stated meetings weekly have been kept up in our church now for six months—well attended—and at most of these for months the cry for mercy was often heard. The outward manifestations have now nearly ceased, but the work of the Spirit is going on steadily and quietly."

Subjoined in a touching instance of the power of prayer in the case of an entire household. It is supplied by the Rev. George Nesbitt, of Tartaraghan, also in County Armagh:—

"A pious mother, in very humble circumstances, began early last summer to spend an hour daily in prayer for a revival in her family, and in our congregation. Her elder boy, about sixteen, one Monday morning in September, after she had been thus engaged, came off his loom and went to his knees. A few minutes after, her second boy was found on his knees in the *cow-house*. They prayed all that day and the following night. I heard some of their petitions:—' O Lord, come into my hard heart. Put in Thy hand by the hole of the door and open for Thyself, O Jesus. Wash me in the fountain of Thy blood, not my hands and my feet only, but my heart and my soul. O Thou that manifestedst Thyself unto the Hebrew children in the fiery furnace, manifest Thyself unto us this night as our reconciled Father. We have sinned against great mercies and privileges, and are not worthy to be called Thy sons; oh, make us as hired servants!' One found peace on the following day, the other not till Saturday night. Three little brothers have been brought to Christ since. The youngest, who will not be *nine* years of age till March, was on his knees almost *incessantly* for sixteen days. His mother has been asked to pray with him three times after the family retired for the night, and often she lifted him from his knees to persuade him to take food. Not one of the five boys was 'stricken,' and all had been in conviction a number of weeks before their distress was perceived by their parents."

16

The Revival in Donegal, Monaghan, and Cavan

SPACE will not admit of a prolongation of this narrative, and in the case of the three counties which yet remain to be noticed in connection with the progress of the movement, I must select out of the materials at my disposal only a slender portion. The subjoined account of the awakening within his own bounds is written with much simplicity, and yet with a vividness that invests it with a genuine interest, by the Rev. Andrew Long. The place is Monreagh, a rural district in Donegal, a few miles from the city of Derry :—

"In no congregation in this district has the Lord wrought more marvellously. The full tide of the river of God which was passing over our land reached us about the middle of June. We had most interesting meetings in the open air on June 14th and 21st. Another in our church on the 24th, when about twenty souls were savingly impressed. An infidel would have seen that the Holy Spirit alone was working there. One young lad had gone a few yards from the church when he stood and said to his mother, ' Mamma, I cannot go further ; I must turn back and speak to Mr Long.' He remained in the vestry with the others, for a considerable time wrestling with God in deep distress. As yet, however, it was the day of small things with us.

Scenes in the Church.—" On the following Lord's-day, June 26, we enjoyed showers of blessing. God strengthened me as He never did before, for the services of that memorable day; but I know it was in answer to many prayers, and especially those of some of our new-born souls who were heard pleading for me during the day. I never witnessed such deep solemnity. The exercises had almost closed, when one person fell out of her pew upon the aisle, the door being open, and shrieked loudly for mercy. In a few moments about twenty were prostrated in different quarters of the house. And then what a scene ensued! Relatives in groups carrying their stricken ones into the adjoining vestry; multitudes weeping, and the whole congregation moved and excited as if the judgment-day had come. I came down from the pulpit in order to keep the passage to the vestry clear, when just behind me, a young female, a member of the congregation, whose heart the Lord had touched in Derry, lifted up her hands, and in an unearthly voice, addressed the assembly, thanking God that the flood of God's Spirit had not passed us by unvisited—telling of *her* love to Jesus, and entreating those who were looking at salvation from afar, to come to the precious Saviour and be reconciled to God. *She* would not take ten thousand worlds for Jesus. I—not knowing what to do —permitted her to address the congregation for a few minutes. The heavenly light which had been imparted to her mind beamed through her countenance. And she who, a few days previous, would not and could not have ventured to speak one word for Christ, was not ashamed now to lift up her voice like a trumpet, and out of the abundance of her heart to urge the thoughtless sinner to fly from the wrath to come. Her simple address was certainly the most touching and telling appeal to which I have ever listened; and the entire scene was unlike one of earth. Many a stout and stubborn heart that had hitherto resisted the Holy Ghost was compelled to yield. I had often read of the prostration of the convicted leper, but I never witnessed a *fac-simile* of it until that day. A strong young man was on his knees in deep mental agony, refusing to be comforted, pressing his very face upon the dust of the vestry floor, and in this position he remained for several hours. In every part of the church there were broken-hearted penitents on their knees pleading for mercy; and at the same time not a few hardened sinners were looking on and wondering. But at length the feelings of many gave way, and the big tears rolled down many a wrinkled cheek.

In the Open Air.—" In the evening I held a meeting in the open air about a mile from the church, and addressed an assembly of two thousand. There were three converts from Derry present,—a porter, a tailor, and a sailor. The former said, in his own tender, simple, touching manner, ' I am but a poor porter, earning nine shillings a week for drawing my handcart through the streets of Derry, but I would not change my situation for that of the richest among *yez* if you have not got Christ.' The tailor, in offering up a short prayer, said, ' Lord, have mercy on those poor sinners who do not care one *happorth* about their souls.'

In the Church again.—" At this meeting a few were awakened, and at its close a great number flocked to the church, though it was now nine o'clock, and remained there till next morning. There was one great-grandmother present, and several grandparents were rejoicing over their penitent offspring. And, oh, the burning words of some who had obtained peace as they addressed God in prayer! It was a joyous time. The countenance of one girl was truly angelic, as, looking up, she poured forth her gratitude to God, and gave Him the glory, crying, 'Precious Jesus! lovely Jesus! sweeter to me than honey and the honeycomb.' Similar expressions might have been heard ringing through the sanctuary at intervals, as the parties found peace and joy in believing. One person aged fifty-five years, arose, and said in a loud voice that he never had a family altar in his house, but he would go home and erect one, and keep it up till he would die. It is now nine months since, and he is still faithful to his vow. One little girl of eleven said she would not take a hundred guineas for her interest in Christ, no, nor a thousand, for Christ was better to her than them all. Another girl on obtaining peace offered up a sweet prayer in the presence of a multitude. She first gave God the glory for what He had done for her soul, and then pleaded earnestly for me; and many others have done in like manner. I have frequently overheard them wrestling with God on my behalf.

Abiding Fruits.—" I am happy to say that, in so far as known to our session and myself, there has not yet been one case of backsliding. There may not be that intense ardour which was apparent on 'the day of their espousals;' yet I believe there is no real diminution of love to Christ, but an accession of higher and deeper feelings. The change in the moral aspect of society here is truly marvellous."

In Donoughmore, in the same county, there was a great awakening, followed by an entire change in the moral aspects of society—a change not confined to those who were themselves brought to a knowledge of the truth, but extending to almost all residing in the locality.

"I have been much surprised, says the Rev. A. Caldwell, at the outpouring of prayer resulting from the revival. How different the prayers from those of former times! how original the ideas and the language in which they were expressed! I was deeply moved on one occasion by hearing a female, in a public meeting, use the following words—' O Lord, I know the devil is no stronger now than he was, but Thou well knowest he is a thousand times busier with me than he ever was. O Lord, for my Saviour's sake, command him to leave me, that I may have peace.'

"With respect to the permanency of the work, thank God, I am able to say that, out of more than two hundred cases which have come under my observation, I do not know one who professed to be savingly converted who is not still maintaining a consistent walk and conversation. I know persons who were not only stricken, but heavily prostrated, who seem more hardened and wicked than ever. There are only very few of these, and not one of them ever even professed to be converted."

COUNTY MONAGHAN

Impressions of a Visit.—The Rev. H. M. Waddell, missionary, first in Jamaica, and subsequently in Western Africa, in referring to his unwillingness to traverse the revival districts, lest too many visitors should prove injurious to the young converts, adds, "But when I heard that it was making progress through my native county, *Monaghan*, which tourists and travellers seldom visit, where I could see old friends and fulfil old promises, by preaching for some of the overworked ministers, I thought that I might, in the way of duty, go and see that great thing which the Lord has brought to pass in our days.

In the Country.—After narrating several interviews with ministers and others, Mr Waddell proceeds to state that he went among the hamlets and small farmhouses in "an-out-of-the-way" rural district, there to converse with some of the families in which the revival had appeared with some of its more remarkable effects. "At one place," he says, "seven young women hastily came in from their field labours to meet me, one running to call another. They had all but one been struck, though at different times and in different places; and, as usual, after a period of prostration had found peace and comfort by that greatest and best of all names, the name of Jesus. One of them was a recent case, and she was still weak. They gave a simple account of what had happened to them: sudden and uncontrollable emotion, with fears, and faintness, and depression; a load at the heart; their sins and their souls; recovery, after hours of anguish, by faith in Jesus the Saviour. It did not for so far seem unintelligible. They had all been Sabbath scholars, and some of them communicants. The Spirit of the Lord made short work with them. The experience of years was compressed into hours; and their conversion, like the outburst of a tornado on the African coast after a long calm, was the explosion of accumulated and condensed forces, brief and violent, breaking down all before it.

The subjects on which I preached were not of an exciting character, or delivered in any exciting manner. In both respects I might say they were rather the opposite—simple gospel sermons. I had preached the same discourses in Scotland, without seeing any unusual effect produced. I must, therefore, attribute the effect on this occasion to some other cause than my preaching. What the 'proper hysteric tone and gesture' may be, which some hostile or frivolous writers allude to, I know not. Certainly mine on these occasions whether bad or good, were just what they have usually been, and in themselves, I presume, as ineffective as ever."

The town of Monaghan shared in the blessing, and the Rev. John Bleckley, the much-respected pastor of the Presbyterian church, has been refreshed after a lengthened ministry, by the happy results that he has witnessed. In the course of about five months after the commencement of the revival, he preached no less than a hundred and thirty times!

A few miles distant from the county town is Newbliss, in which the movement began in August. The immediate occasion was the visit of two lay-agents from county Antrim. " In their addresses," says the Rev. R. Dunlop, who supplies the information, " there was not the slightest attempt to arouse an undue excitement or produce a merely temporary enthusiasm. The cases he mentions and the results of the movement resemble those so familiar elsewhere.

COUNTY CAVAN

It was about the middle of the month of August when this county, one of the most distant from the centre whence the work of revival radiated forth in all directions, was visited by the gracious influence. Several of the principal towns, as Cavan, Killesandra, Cootehill, and Bailieborough, felt its power. In the neighbourhood of the last-named district there was a very extensive awakening. The circumstances were briefly these :—

On the 8th of August last two young men, now students in divinity in connection with the Presbyterian Church, visited the first congregation of Bailieborough, of which for many years their father has been the respected pastor, and addressed a meeting there. Having intimated that they would narrate, on the evening following, what they had witnessed in the north, they had an unusually large attendance, when the usual results were witnessed. A few evenings later the green around the church was thronged by groups of persons, now returning thanks for some near relative or friend who had found the Saviour, now in earnest supplication that light might break in upon the darkness of some distressed soul, and peace be found by some troubled conscience.

Special meetings were immediately established in the Presbyterian churches, and the neighbourhood was deeply moved. The hands of ministers were so full that had they not received timely aid, they must have been altogether overborne. Happily a Young Men's Society, which had met for some time for religious purposes, came to their aid; while the two students found abundant occupation throughout all the adjacent districts.

There is a district not far from Killesandra, in the same county, named Drumkeeran, of which no notice has been taken in any of the reports of the revival, and where certainly a most extraordinary and in some respects unprecedented movement has taken place. The young minister of the Presbyterian church, the Rev. Samuel Patrick, has been so enfeebled by excessive labour, that he has been unable to furnish any statement on the subject. During the first week in October, about which time the place was visited, he never laid himself down to sleep. The meetings which were held nightly in the church were so exciting, and the interest of the people such, that they could not be prevailed on to disperse till the following morning; while during all the day anxious inquirers and others demanded the incessant attention of the pastor.

Among the earliest visitors to the north of Ireland,

after the commencement of the revival, was the Rev. F. F. Trench, prebendary of St Patrick's, Dublin, and rector of Newtown, near Kells, in the province of Leinster. For many years the name of this devoted minister (the son of the last Archbishop of Tuam), has been well known in connection with every evangelistic movement in the Episcopal Church. After his visit northwards he published some account of his impressions in the pubilc newspapers, thus spreading an interest in the movement in many quarters in the South and West of Ireland. During the winter he has been called to take a part in conducting meetings in some of the parishes in county Cavan, adjacent to his own in Meath; and from a statement issued from private circulation, which I have his permission to use, I select the following cases as still further illustrative of the character and progress of the work in the former county:—

"There are many residing in the province of Leinster who are and have been praying that 'the revival' may 'reach even unto them;' and it will be deeply interesting to all such to know that this unprecedented movement, in its full force and power, is at their doors. I have extreme gratification in being able to state that, within an easy morning's ride from my own house, I have witnessed as interesting scenes, and have heard of as remarkable cases of conversion, as any of those which I witnessed or heard of higher up in the North.

"Very lately I spent a Sunday in a neighbouring parish in the county of Cavan for the purpose of ascertaining facts. I had heard that several persons had been struck in Presbyterian churches, and in the parish church, some at open-air meetings, many more at their own houses, in the fields, and while engaged at their ordinary occupations. On visiting this parish, and making inquiry at the curate, and also at the Presbyterian ministers, I found that the facts were quite as remarkable as had been stated to me, and that the awakening had not been confined to the lower classes, but that men of wealth and respectability, and considerable education, had been led to feel their sins, as well as persons in the lower class and of the most abandoned character, male and female. I found that a large and lucrative business in the sale of spirituous liquors had been renounced for conscience' sake, serving as a strong testimony of the sincerity of the merchant who did so. I found that persons had been convinced of their sins in an *overwhelming* manner in all sorts of places,—churches, meeting-houses, parlours, shops, bed-rooms, and in ' byres ' or *cow-houses*. And I also ascertained that these conversions had been attended with a great variety of the most remarkable circumstances, and the best moral results."

The rector of two united parishes, one in County Cavan and the other in Meath, writes :—

The Moral Results.—" The following occurrence took place between three brothers, two of whom had been for eight years on bad terms with the other, because of his having taken a farm which they conceived they had a right to. (Those who know the murderous results which so frequently attend agrarian quarrels in Ireland, will know how to estimate it.) The man who had taken the farm, while engaged in family worship, became unhappy. and on his wife asking him the cause, he turned to Matt. v. 23, 24—' If thy brother hath aught against thee,' &c., and, pointing to the passage, said, ' That is the cause.' His wife replied, ' Then why don't you act upon it ? ' ' Will you come with me ? ' ' I will ; ' upon which they both rose, and went with the literally open Bible to their brother's house, which was close by. He met them at the door. His brother then said, that since the grace of God had reached his heart, he could not be happy while on bad terms with him, and pointed to the above-mentioned passage in the open Bible which he held in his hand. On reading it, his brother was affected to tears, and kissed him. He then asked him if he would like to make friends with the other brother, and that if so, he would send for him. The other brother was accordingly sent for; the same Scripture was shown to him; he also was affected to tears, embraced his brother, and a similar reconciliation took place with him on the spot. These three brothers have since continued on good terms; two out of three now partake of the Lord's Supper, which only one of them did before, and all three have commenced the practice of family worship. The following is perhaps a scarcely less perfect example:—A convert said, after returning from the first fair he had been at after his conversion, that ' he never was so hard put to it as to sell the cow without telling a lie about the milk.' Several Roman Catholics living in Protestant families have been deeply ' affected.' I conversed with one most intelligent convert, now regularly attending the church; and impressions tending to good have unquestionably been made on many others. For instance, the following conversation relative to certain young men who had been converted under most remarkable circumstances occurred between some Roman Catholic labourers in the employment of a farmer, who repeated it to me:—' ——, didn't you say the revival was the devil's work?' 'No, I didn't.' ' Then, what did you say?' ' I said I couldn't understand it at all.' ' Then, some of you said it was the devil's work; and I say it can't be, for see ——, and others,—

the devil wouldn't bring such a change over them ; and what's more, even we ourselves, when we see the change in them, can't sin as we used to do ; and, signs on it, we haven't the penance we used to have ! ' The respectable farmer who heard this conversation, told me that he was so affected by the testimony to the power of religion which these Roman Catholics gave one to another, that he was obliged to leave them."

Here we must close this portion of our narrative of the progress of the movement in Ulster. There is reason to believe, however, that it has not been altogether confined to our northern province, but has, to a greater or less extent, been taking a direction southwards. In the county of Longford, which is in Leinster, there are not wanting indications of its presence ; and there too the brethren report that some of a higher class in the community have been brought under the gracious influence.

In the metropolis itself there have been evidence of an unusual interest in the things of God. Meetings for prayer and fellowship on a scale unknown before have been lately held ; and in the minds of the Protestant community there is a growing anticipation of better things to come.

In Munster also, although there is not a plenteous rain, yet drops of the shower are falling upon the pastures of the wilderness. In the city of Limerick, in particular, there would seem to be the commencement of a time of hallowed visitation. In the Presbyterian church, under the ministry of the Rev. David Wilson, there have been delightful evidences of a deepening spirituality ; and, especially at communion seasons, there has been sweet and refreshing Christian fellowship. An evangelical union for prayer, into which the ministers of the Independent and Wesleyan churches have cordially entered, is in efficient operation, and the best impression has been produced on the public mind by the edifying spectacle. On the second week in January last, when the concert for prayer was general, the several congregations with their pastors were seen to flow together to one place at special services, and to meet for prayer and praise as one body in Christ. In the Independent chapel there are held nightly and protracted meetings, at which many are represented to have been brought to the enjoyment of perfect peace. And so this ancient city is opening its gates to that Celestial Visitant, who, in whatever heart or home He finds an entrance, brings with him a satisfying and abiding joy.

As these sheets are passing through the press, I have received, from the Rev. J. Denham Smith of Kingstown, a little volume (just published), in which he narrates the progress of a remarkable work of revival, not only among his own flock, but among a class of men who have too often been unhappy wanderers from the fold—the sailors of the port. The crews of the express boats *Telegraph* and *Cambria*, plying across the Channel, are especially alluded to as having become the subjects of a gracious influence. The following extract is deeply interesting :—

"It would be impossible to describe all the happy scenes on board these boats.

"Lord's-day, December 3, will be long remembered. It was the day when Roman Catholic Kingstown was assembled in sympathy for the Pope. There was within sound of that meeting one in the open air, convened for

THE REVIVAL IN DONEGAL, ETC. 191

prayer. There, on the bended knee, and beneath the chill skies of December, the newly-awakened and converted were pouring forth their warm, loving prayers, that God in mercy to us would send forth His Spirit into the hearts of all—Protestant, Nonconformist, and Romanist alike. This meeting was held at the New Pier. There was no prearrangement. Providence alone had driven it to the open air. At the usual hour for Divine service on board, it became evident that hundreds could not avail themselves of the ordinary accommodation. For long months the saloon, passages, and stairs of the steamships have been too strait for the crowds that assemble. By request, the whole mass of the people resorted to the deck, which was partly covered and partly open. The scene on board and on shore was one of great interest. There was no noisy excitement, no declamatory violence, no cold formality, no pharisaic sense of sect or party, but one calm and continued manifestation of the Spirit of God in prayer. An earnest and solemn appeal was made by one of the speakers, on the value of the human soul, the brevity of time, the nearness of eternity, of heaven and hell; on the value of the knowledge of the Lord Jesus Christ, and the preciousness of its present experience, as well for life as for death. A letter to the captain was read, and a short sermon preached. At the call for prayer for the outpouring of the Holy Ghost on Kingstown, Dublin, and the towns and villages around, one after another, sailors and landsmen, in calm and orderly succession, commenced to pray. Some who prayed were the newly-converted. Never were more earnest supplications uttered, under similar circumstances, in Kingstown. . . .

" On the 11th of the same month a still more remarkable day was given to the friends of prayer on board the

Llewellyn city of Dublin steamship, as she lay alongside the quay, near the railway station. The service on board this boat commenced about three o'clock. The foredeck was filled, and a large company of all ranks and creeds ranked themselves along the pier, who listened with marked attention to the addresses and prayers. A Roman Catholic priest was present during the sermon on the words, ' *Ye must be born again.*' This service concluded at four o'clock, when the *Llewellyn* crew joined the crew of the express boat, and sang hymns together, one of the *Llewellyn* sailors bursting forth into prayer. The weather was peculiarly favourable for this open-air service, and many came away rejoicing at what the Lord was doing. A minister of the Established Church offered up prayer at the close. It was mentioned at the noon prayer-meeting, by the president of that meeting, that he had seen more of the *distinct manifestation of the Spirit's work in Kingstown* since the previous Sabbath that he had seen in his whole life before, excepting the last three months, when the revival may be said to have commenced there.

"The happy condition of these sailor-brethren is thus characteristically referred to by one who was lately crossing with them—an observant passenger—the Rev. C. H. Spurgeon, in his discourse, January 26, 1860:—

"'The most pleasing thing I have seen is this.' Hervey once said, ' Each floating ship a floating hell.' Of all classes of men, the sailor has been supposed to be the man least likely to be reached by the gospel. In crossing over from Holyhead to Dublin and back, I spent the most pleasant hour that I ever spent. The first vessel that I entered, I found my hands very heartily shaken by the sailors. I thought, ' What can these sailors know of me ? ' and they were calling me ' *brother*.'

Of course I felt that I was their brother too; but I did not know how they came to talk to me in that way. It was not generally the way for sailors to call ministers brother; and when I made the inquiry, 'What makes you so kind?' 'Why,' said one, 'because I love your Master the Lord Jesus.' I inquired, and found that out of the whole crew there were but three unconverted men; that though the most of them had been before without God and without Christ, yet by a visitation of the Spirit of God they had all been converted. My heart was lifted up with joy, to think of a ship being made a floating church—a very Bethel for God. When I came back by another ship I did not expect to see the like, but it was precisely the same. The same work had been going on. They told me a story of a gentleman who stood laughing when a hymn was being sung, and one of the men proposed that they should pray for him. They did, and that man was suddenly smitten down, and began on the quay to cry for mercy, and plead with God for pardon. 'Ah! sir,' said the sailors, 'we have the best proof that there is a God here, for we have seen this crew marvellously brought to a knowledge of the truth; and here we are, joyful and happy men, serving the Lord.'"

17

The Revival and the Roman Catholics

FOR the last three quarters of a century the several Protestant churches in Ireland have been engaged in efforts for the evangelisation of the Roman Catholics of that country. At the period of the famine, about sixty-four years ago, when the hand of the Almighty lay heavily on the land, a door of access was opened to those districts which, in the south and west, had suffered so severely from the calamitous visitation. Agencies were thenceforward employed, and enterprises undertaken, some of them on a large and expensive scale, for the dissemination of Protestant truth ; and there is reason to believe that for some years subsequently many were led to renounce the system of Romanism, and to embrace the tenets of a purer faith. Of late there has been comparatively little to report of success in this department, unless whatever may have been realised among the youthful portion of the population through those industrial and educational appliances which, especially in Connaught, have done much to elevate the general community. The great awakening, however, by which a merely nominal Protestantism has been made to glow with a new life, has brought Divine truth into vital contact with the minds of many who have heretofore been immersed in Romish ignorance ; and has guided along the upward path many who were groping amid the thickest darkness. Some of these are noble specimens of Christian consist-

REVIVAL AND THE ROMAN CATHOLICS 195

ency and steadfastness, who, amid many trials and seductions, have already proved that they count all things but loss for the excellency of the knowledge of Jesus Christ.

It is impossible to compute the number of this interesting class of converts. In many cases, as stated in the returns with which I have been favoured, individuals have been spirited away from their respective neighbourhoods, and placed out of the reach of those influences under which they had given hopeful evidence of being brought. In others, and these perhaps the majority of instances, the first transient impressions were speedily effaced, and the parties so affected returned to their former spiritual allegiance. The practice too generally adopted of making public every case of secession from Rome, inspired its votaries with fresh vigilance, and alarmed the priesthood into the employment of all their artifices by which to win back the neophytes, and to assert over them their own exclusive jurisdiction. To this it is to be added that, knowing little of gospel truth before they became alive to the importance of eternal things, even the best of those who " came out " from the old system by which they were enslaved, required much careful training and instruction before they could be admitted to the participation of Christian privileges.

It is wonderful, however, how, notwithstanding the operation of such varied and adverse influences, so many were intelligently enabled to relinquish their ecclesiastical relationships, and to embrace the simple truth as it is in Jesus; how all at once they turned away from human mediators, and, with loud cries for mercy, did homage to the only name by which the sinner can be saved; how, in despite of social ties and petty persecutions, they persevered in waiting upon God in a form and manner which not long before they would have utterly abjured ; and how so large a number have been enabled to witness a good confession before many witnesses, and by the quiet force of an exemplary demeanour to stop the mouths of gainsayers.

In the returns alluded to, I have received the most satisfactory assurances, after making full deduction for all dubious cases, of the genuine conversion, so far as man can judge, of several hundreds of Romanists, and that only in connection with a single section of the Protestant church. The following selected instances are taken from the several communications with which I have been furnished :—

The Crimean Soldier.—The first case is that of one who gave good evidence of genuine conversion, both in life and death. It is supplied by the Rev. Joseph Barkley, of Carnmoney, County Antrim. " He was a soldier, who lost his health by exposure to cold in the trenches at the Crimea, and was discharged in consequence. He returned to his native place an enfeebled and broken-down man, though still in the prime of life, but without pension or other means of support. Two years ago he was supposed to be at the point of death, and was told by both doctor and priest that he had but a short time to live ; on which the poor fellow burst into tears, and besought the Lord to spare him a little longer, ' to make his soul,' as he expressed it. His prayer was heard, his health in a measure restored, and his soul saved in the following manner :—A young man, who had himself been brought to Christ during the revival, set his heart on his conversion. He spoke to him about his soul, and, as the soldier had never learned to read, he spent night after night instructing him out of the Scriptures in the way of salvation, and uniting with him in prayer. The other

REVIVAL AND THE ROMAN CATHOLICS 197

converts were also exceedingly attentive to him, meeting almost every night for prayer in his little cabin, which consisted of a single apartment, and supplying him out of their own scanty means with the necessaries of life. They loved him as a brother, and it was a very beauteous spectacle to see the deep interest they took in his welfare. God at length crowned their efforts with success. The Spirit was given in answer to prayer, and he was enabled to rejoice in God his Saviour; and seldom has it been our lot to witness, even among Protestants, deeper piety, or more unfaltering faith in the finished work of Christ, than was exhibited by the Crimean soldier prior to his death."

Two Females and a Male Convert.—These cases are supplied by the Rev. F. Buick, of Ahoghill, in the same county. " Several Roman Catholics in this district who felt the revival, are keeping firm to Christ, and are growing in Divine things. Some of them, who were bigoted in their former faith, hostile to the truth, and far from what they ought to be, are now amongst the loveliest specimens of a living Christianity. With the change of their hearts, their views and characters, there is a most pleasing change in their outward person. The love of Jesus, of His Word and ordinances, is now intense. One of the same persuasion, brought up in the glens of Antrim, was dark and ignorant and gloomy indeed. She was brought under conviction, and led to Jesus. Forthwith she was severed from her former faith, and light gradually began to cast its bright radiance on her features. She felt very powerful bodily manifestations, being unable to speak for several days; but during this period she made rapid advances in knowledge. When directed to Jesus—when she got glimpses of His love—when persuaded of His willingness to save even the chief of sinners—and when assured that, believing on Him, she should not perish, but have everlasting life, her countenance assumed a heavenly appearance of light and beauty, filled with joy unspeakable, and full of glory. She is now an earnest worshipper in a Presbyterian church, and of the reality of her change her neighbours entertain no doubt. Another woman of the same persuasion, who was a regular bigot in her way, has been converted in the revival. Her hold of Rome has been broken ; and her prayers for her former guides are most earnest and special. She is in terror lest her people should force her to return home, well knowing that they would confine her, in order to compel her to go back to her former faith —but against this she seems fully determined. A young man, brought up in the same religion, happened to attend worship in our church on a Sabbath when there was a powerful movement among the congregation. Many were stricken, and most of the worshippers on that day were moved to tears. After his return from the house of God, and when in a family where the revival had entered, he was stricken ; and when visited he was found pouring out a stream of earnest prayers to Jesus, as the Saviour of sinners. On a Bible being brought into his hand, he said he would ' never let it go.' Thenceforth he has been an anxious inquirer. His progress in Divine things is astonishing. His gifts of prayer and praise and exhortation are truly wonderful ; and his delight by night and day now is in continuing to exercise them, and in trying to win sinners to the Saviour. His path is like that of the just, shining more and more unto the perfect day."

An Aged Female.—The next case is one which also occurred in the county Antrim. Going to visit one day with a brother minister, Mr Simpson of Portrush was met by a young woman, who thus accosted him :—

REVIVAL AND THE ROMAN CATHOLICS 199

" Mr Simpson, when are you going again to visit Widow S—— ? "

" I am just on my way there ; have you any message for me ? "

With quivering lip and tearful eye she walked along, and made no reply. The two ministers followed in silence after the weeper, not wishing to interfere with the sacredness of her grief. By and by Mr Simpson came up, and addressed her :—

" Please who are you ? and have you anything particular to say to me ? "

" Oh, I am wife of A. C——, and the old woman was very uneasy in her mind since she heard you at Widow S——'s house, and wants you to go back again."

The " old woman " referred to was so wedded to the Romish system that she had been known to rush out of a house in which a Presbyterian minister was about to kneel in prayer.

" You don't mean to tell me that *she* wishes to hear me, do you ? "

" It's true enough, sir. She bade me call on you, and inquire when you would be up ; but I didn't know how I could even go to your door after what I have done."

" Why, what's the matter ? what have you done ? "

" Oh ! I was once a Presbyterian, but married a Roman Catholic, and have gone to mass with him, and had my child christened by the priest."

" Bad enough."

" Yes, very bad ; but of one thing I'll assure you, if God spares my health and life, my foot shall never cross a mass-house door again."

A fresh gush of tears came, and she sobbed convulsively. After a little quiet, Mr Simpson, who himself was not a little moved, invited her to come over with her aged relative to the house in question, to which she readily assented. The place was filled, as usual when a minister was seen to enter any house on such an errand. The portion read was the 103rd Psalm; and in the remarks made it was particularly urged that each should be led to ask that they might be enabled to say, " Bless the Lord, O *my* soul." The exercise in due time terminated, and the minister retired.

Calling after nightfall at another house in the neighbourhood, Mr Simpson found that its principal inmates had gone to pray with the Roman Catholic old woman who so earnestly desired to hear him in the morning, as she had been very unhappy. In the after-part of the day she was outside her little cottage, when a perfect flood of light, as she imagined, bathed the dwelling; and rushing in, she raised a wild cry for mercy, and fainted away. It was not to the Virgin that she poured forth her plaint, but to Him who alone can hear and give deliverance.

At eleven o'clock that night, the foot of the Presbyterian minister crossed her threshold, and as soon as her eye fell upon him, she exclaimed, " Oh! I *can* say, sir, before I sleep, ' Bless the Lord, O my soul.' " Beside her on the bed lay an open Bible, the symbol of her new faith and hope, though she could not read a syllable. The 103rd Psalm, at her request, was again read, and thanks were offered to Him from whom she had obtained mercy.

The younger woman, who had borne the message of the morning, seeing the change so divinely wrought, especially on the unhappy temper of the aged female, was convinced also. " Both have since been received," says Mr Simpson, " into the communion of the Presbyterian Church, and are, so far as man can judge, walking

REVIVAL AND THE ROMAN CATHOLICS

in the commandments and ordinances of the Lord blameless."

The Boy who Battled for his Liberty.—This case is thus introduced by the Rev. James White of Carrickfergus :—

"We have had some interesting cases of awakening among Roman Catholics. One young lad, who had been brought under conviction while a servant in the employment of a hearer of mine, has been spirited away I know not where. Poor boy! I fear it has been made impossible for him to follow the convictions of his own awakened conscience. Another boy, after braving a storm before which many an older head would have quailed, has battled successfully for his liberty."

The latter case is one of peculiar interest. The name of the lad is Costello, and the circumstances are well known in Ulster through the public press, as brought out in a judicial investigation ; as the result of which his own mother, who had grievously maltreated the youth, was obliged to give security to keep the peace towards him. He had been a subject of the awakening in his native place, and had received such treatment as is too often shared by those who assert their independence of the yoke of Rome. In his evidence before the bench of magistrates, and in a letter subsequently in a Liverpool publication, Costello made, in substance, the following statement :—

"On the evening of the 3rd July, my mother having, along with others, taken me home by force, they all began together to try to influence me. One said I should be put behind the fire and burned ; others attempted also to put me in bodily fear. A person who was stopping in the house, more reasonable than the rest, said to them, ' You cannot resist the Almighty. If the boy desires to go to meeting (the Presbyterian worship), let him ; if he wants to go to chapel (the Roman Catholic), let him go.' But they would not consent to that at all. Searching my clothes after I had gone to bed, they found a little hymn-book in my pocket, which they burned. My mother came into the room in which I lay, not yet asleep, but pretending to be so, and sprinkled me with holy water. When I awoke in the morning, I began to sing little hymns which I had learnt out of the book they burned. My mother bade me desist, but I persevered until she gave me my own way. I then got a New Testament, and began to read in bed; whereupon one of two ladies who had come in said that it should be burned too; the other said, No; she would rather bury it. Again, when they had left, I sang some hymns; whereupon my mother seized a heavy stick, and began to do as she had been instructed by the priest, who, when sent for the day before to see me, did not come, but sent a message to them to beat me with a stick, and throw a bucket of cold water over me. I strove, as well as I could, to defend myself, but after a struggle I sank resistless on the bed. I was sorely hurt; but I blamed the priest, not my mother.

"After a while my strength recruited, and the priest came. He began to laugh and scoff at the revival—speaking of a mustard blister and the asylum as the best cure for it. I quoted part of the New Testament in the second chapter of the Acts, when he immediately said, 'How do you know that that is the word of God? If you prove to me that any part of the Bible is the word of God, I'll give you £200.' 'Well, sir,' I said, 'I can't prove anything; but since you don't believe the Scriptures, I need not talk to you.' The holy water being run out, my mother asked him to make some more; and then he spent some fifteen minutes at the holy water at the bed-side. So I got rid of him. Others coming in, one asked me to say my prayers, which I said on till I came to the 'Hail Mary!' which I skipped, and came to the apostles' creed. 'Hail Mary!' cries the other. 'No,' said I, 'no "Hail Mary!" for me;' and with that my mother began again with the stick, at the bidding of this woman; but I forgive her, for she acted as she was told. In the scuffle the candle was blown out, and on its being lighted again, the person before mentioned drew me towards her, and made me say the Popish prayers. If I had not said them, they would have all but killed me; and with this I conclude. I have not penned half of the things against them, for they have gone out of my mind."

It is gratifying to know, as stated by Mr White, that the victim of such cruelties has escaped out of the hands of his tormentors, and is now receiving the benefit of instruction in one of our principal educational institutions.

The story of the *Lost Token* is thus related by Mr Matthew Patteson of Edinburgh, to whom it was communicated when on a visit to his native country at the period of the awakening:—

"A Roman Catholic woman returning from the town of B——, in the County Antrim, on a Saturday evening, saw something shining on the road. She had never seen anything like it before. 'I don't know what it is,' she said; 'but it is for *luck* any way,' and she put it in her pocket. Next day she looked at it, and read, 'This do in remembrance of me' (Luke xxii. 19). She thought on these words—what could they mean? It must be something about Christ. On Tuesday night she was prostrated in her own house, under deep conviction of sin, and cried to the Lord Jesus to have mercy on her soul. Her husband proposed to send for the priest. 'No, no,' said she, 'no one can do me good but Jesus Christ.' Her husband still persisting, she said, 'If you send for any one, send for the Presbyterian minister.' He was sent for, and on arriving he saw in a moment what was the matter, and said, ' The blood of Jesus Christ, God's Son, cleanseth us from all sin.' ' Neither is there salvation in any other, for there is none other name under heaven given among men whereby we must be saved.' ' Him that cometh unto me I will in nowise cast out.' He offered up a short and simple prayer, and left. Some days after, he saw her again. She was quite composed. He asked her, ' Had she been at any meeting ?' ' No.' ' What, then, led you to think of your sins ? ' She mentioned the above particulars, and drawing something from her pocket, added, ' It was this did it all.' Looking at it, he said, ' This is one of my communion tokens ; some one returning from the Saturday sermon must have dropped it.' He explained its use as a sign of church-membership, and that they were returned by the parties when seated at the communion-table, adding, ' We have a limited number of them, and are anxious they should not fall into wrong hands ; and as it is of no use to you, I will feel obliged to you for it.' ' Oh, no,' she replied, ' I cannot give it you. I will never part with it till I put it into your own hand sitting at the communion-table.' "

The Drunken Beggar is mentioned in a few words by the Rev. J. M. Rogers of Kilrea, County Derry :—

" One of our converts was a Papist, a beggar and a drunkard. He persists in attending most regularly our public services and prayer - meetings — though, on principle, we have not given him till now any congregational aid. He never takes intoxicating drink of any kind, though offered money to use the smallest quantity. He is proof, as I believe, through grace, against ridicule, temptation, and persecution."

One who had Married a Presbyterian finds a narrator of

her interesting story in the Rev. Alexander Minniss of Saltersland, County Derry :—

"S—— K—— was married to a dissolute man, whose name she bears, some years since. Her husband was a nominal Presbyterian, but by his godless habits gave melancholy evidence of the utter absence of all religion. His wife was brought up a strict Roman Catholic, to which system all her connections belong. After her marriage she occasionally attended public worship in our congregation. Her presence there did not result from any love to the truth, or any change in her religious views, but merely from a slavish fear of her husband, by whom she was sometimes constrained to attend. This was still further evinced by the fact that when I sometimes called at their house, I could easily observe that she had very little regard either for me or my religious principles. Matters went on in this way for a year or two after their marriage, when eventually they gave up all connection with us, and sank into a state of absolute heathenism, both alike neglecting all ordinances, the husband in particular becoming addicted to the vilest habits.

"Early in June last, she who is more particularly the subject of the present notice was stricken down at a meeting in the neighbourhood, though not conducted by me. I had not seen her for two or three years before that time. It seems that when visited in this way, those who were about her offered to send for a priest or any clergyman of any denomination she might desire. She stated that her wishes were that I should be sent for. With as much promptitude as possible I visited her habitation, and found her weak in body, and much distressed in mind. After a considerably lengthened interview, I left her in an improved condition, not only in relation to mental peace, but even apparently in regard to bodily strength.

"From that time forward she began to attend with the utmost regularity our Sabbath services, evening meetings, and classes for the instruction of the young. She was grossly ignorant, not having been taught even to read. Her desire for knowledge appeared very earnest, and her progress satisfactory.

"Matters went on in this way until about the end of August, when, apparently in great anxiety, she came to me one Sabbath morning, to say that she desired to speak with me. Her object was to narrate to me a dream that she had had on the previous night. She dreamed that four angelic-looking beings came into the room where she was, and sang a portion of the 40th Psalm, and enjoined her to persevere in the course she was pursuing. I gave her what instruction on the subject I considered salutary—telling her that although we are not to regard dreams as prophetic, yet God may even in sleep superintend the imagination for good and useful purposes, and endeavouring practically to apply the truth in her case. On the Wednesday following she came to me again, and stated that during the preceding night she had had a vision similar to the other, in which she was enjoined to come to me and desire to be baptized. From that time she became intensely anxious to receive the ordinance of baptism. Her views on the subject were perfectly correct. She often stated to me that it was not owing to a belief that it would save her soul that she desired to be baptized ; but owing to the fact that having had the ceremony administered according to the form of the Church of Rome, she had never been scripturally baptized. For some weeks she waited carefully on instruction. I was pleased, and even astonished at her progress. At length I examined her in the presence of the session, after our Sabbath service, and having received their approval, on the succeeding Sabbath, in the presence of the assembled congregation, administered the solemn rite. After that, at our communion in the month of November, I had the peculiar gratification of admitting her for the first time to the Lord's table, in company with a considerable number of the young of our charge, who had made a consistent profession of having received a saving change.

"It is with great gratification that I am able to add, that the profession of this woman is still marked by the most unswerving consistency. I believe she bears the most unmistakable fruits of genuine godliness. Her husband, who was one of the most reckless men in the whole community, has now been completely changed. He also was admitted to the Lord's Supper for the first time on the last occasion. I believe the influence of her example and admonitions was blessed by God as the instrumentality in leading to this change. Owing to imprudent habits during past years, they had contracted debt. Their creditors were disposed, I believe, to give up their case as hopeless. Since this change, however, by great self-sacrifice they seem determined to act honestly. But with all this outward pressure and straitened circumstances, I have been astonished at the liberality they seem disposed to exercise in the cause of God. In the population of this district there is a considerable Romish element. Her friends and neighbours bitterly opposed her, and chiefly in regard to the matter of her baptism. Not a few of the careless belonging to all denominations were disposed to scoff. In all cases, when speaking of this cruel treatment, I never saw anything like the existence of a vindictive spirit on her part. Her intimate acquaintances testify how much she delights in prayer. When the imperfect accommodation of her humble home may not have been able to secure her from intrusion, she has been known to retire to some secluded place outside, that there she might more uninterruptedly hold communion with God. In such a situation as this she has been accidentally met with, prostrated before a throne of grace."

The Stammerer Cured.—This is the very remarkable case of a young man, David Creswell, respecting whom I have made the fullest inquiry, and whose history is as follows:—

He had come to Moneymore from Derry, his native place, in very sad plight, seeking work as a stone-mason; and calling at the house of a kind-hearted Wesleyan, his miserable appearance bespoke the sympathy of its owner, who first supplied him with a little food, and afterwards found him suitable employment. Although he had been addicted to intemperance, which had reduced him to his deplorable state of destitution, he conducted himself with much propriety during his sojourn in the place, and there became the subject of a spiritual change, which gave a new direction to his entire future life.

Nothing is more remarkable in the case of Creswell, after his change, than the removal of a natural impediment which at times deprived him of the power of intelligible utterance. So painful was it to witness his ineffectual attempts at articulation, that when he has called at a house to deliver a message, the person whom he addressed has been known to retire to some other apartment on the pretence of business, only to find on his return the messenger still labouring to announce his errand. With this constitutional defect he was also unhappily addicted to the use of profane language, interlarding his discourse, so far as his stammering tongue permitted it, with words of blasphemy. When Moneymore was visited by the awakening, he attended the meetings, but only to hang about the outskirts and indulge in mockery.

On the night of Sabbath, the 19th of June, he was passing at a late hour the open door of a private house in the village, and heard a voice engaged in fervent supplication, and the name of Christ was used in it so impressively and tenderly as to arrest for the moment his errant footsteps. He felt constrained to enter; and in a short time found himself among the domestic group, and uniting with them in the outward form in prayer. When the exercise was ended, and the Rev. Dr Barnett, by whom it was engaged in, rose to depart, he left along with him,— keeping at a distance, to avoid the possibility of personal communication, but resolved to follow him to another dwelling where his presence was desired by some of its anxious inmates. Just then the arrow of the Almighty pierced his spirit, a strange, bewildering terror took possession of him, and he sank prostrate on the earth.

It was now one o'clock on Monday morning, and he was carried into an adjoining house, where he was violently affected for several hours. At five he was able to walk to his own lodging; and there, for nearly a fortnight, he was the subject of many alternations of hope and fear, his bodily weakness incapacitating him for any manner of work. On the 2nd of July he was struck down a second time, and after a deadly conflict he was led, as he believes, to the enjoyment of " perfect peace." Before his change, he had been given to the immoderate use of tobacco, as well as strong drink when he could procure it; but ever since, he has lost all taste for both; while the removal of his physical infirmity came contemporaneously with his spiritual deliverance. From the first moment when he felt himself in the grasp of a higher Power, he refused all priestly aid, and, renouncing the religion of the crucifix for that of the cross, put himself into the hands of Him who, by His own marvellous intervention, had rescued him from temporal and eternal ruin. He has ever since continued to walk worthy of his new-born freedom, and is at this moment at a seminary in England, where he has been placed by the kindness of friends, that he may be educated, and trained for some department of active usefulness.

The Rev. John Knox Leslie, of Cookstown, relates, in the following terms, the case of

The Woman who was a Sinner.—" At the close of one of our prayer-meetings, in summer, a woman I had never known or seen before came up to me, weeping, and expressing an anxious desire to speak to me, as she felt that she was very ignorant of the way of salvation. In company with one of our students, I went out to the country to see her; when I had an opportunity of becoming acquainted with her strange history. She had been cohabiting with a man whose wife is still living for nineteen years, and had nine illegitimate children. Some weeks before the outburst of the revival, she told me, she felt a dreadful weight upon her spirits, which she could not at first understand, but found at last that it was connected with her sin. Her distress of mind became so great that she could neither eat nor sleep; and in the paroxysms of her grief she would rush out of the house, and falling down on her knees behind a hedge, she would call on the Lord for mercy. One day she said to another Romanist woman that she was so distressed that she must go to the priest. ' You need not go,' said the other, ' for he will not listen to your confession, as you are living with a strange man.' ' Well, if he does not receive me, I will go to God Almighty.' The poignancy of her grief continued to increase for weeks. To obtain relief, she had recourse to every Popish expedient—but all in vain. She resolved to pray night and day to the Virgin—but still she

REVIVAL AND THE ROMAN CATHOLICS

received no relief. She then began to draw off from Rome, conversing freely with Protestants on matters of religion, and attended prayer-meetings. She began also to have some obscure glimmerings of the more excellent way of peace and salvation through Jesus Christ. She was groping on in darkness, and the Lord led her by a way that she knew not. She told me that one day, when overwhelmed with agony of soul, she lifted up her heart solely to Christ, when immediately she found relief, and her joy knew no bounds. In the presence of many of the neighbours assembled, she told the man she had so long lived with that her Saviour would not allow her any longer to live with him in sin; that she was yet very ignorant what she should do, but that she was prepared to do whatever the Lord Jesus would require. Her attendance at prayer-meetings and public ordinances in our church has been unremitting. She cannot read, but she is growing rapidly in religious knowledge, and her character and entire conduct are so changed as to exhibit a perfect contrast to what she once was. She continues steadfast and consistent in her religious profession. I said to her one day, ' Could you not be induced once more to pray to the Virgin ? ' ' No,' she said ; ' God has taught me in the school of affliction how vain it is to trust in any creature for salvation.' She is now a member of the Presbyterian Church."

The " Wild Arab " Tamed.—The following interesting case is furnished by the Rev. William J. Patton, of Dromara :—

" In this parish lives a man who earns a livelihood by gathering in rags through the country. In all the district there was none more notorious for wickedness. Every penny he could get was spent in drink ; and often has he pawned the clothes off his back to buy whisky.

Swearing was so familiar that scarcely a word escaped his lips without an oath. Frequently has he been seen lying on the road in a fit of epilepsy, drunk, and after the fit was over, heard to swear so awfully as to make the bystanders tremble lest God should strike him dead.

"When under the influence of drink he was always disposed to fight, and many a time had his poor wife to bear the brunt of the battle. Right well she knew, from hard blows and cruel usage, what it is to be *a drunkard's wife*. His own account of himself is that there was no bad practice of which he was not guilty, except theft and murder; 'and, indeed,' he said to me, 'I did rob and murder my children, for I starved them.'

"He was a Romanist, and a very bigoted one—the more so, perhaps, that his wife was a Protestant—and he had never been in a Protestant place of worship in his life. He was, moreover, as ignorant as any priest could desire—not able to read a word.

"Such was this ignorant, Popish, drunken, swearing, fighting, wife-beating ragman.

"When the revival began here, he mocked, as might have been expected. Speaking one day of a person who had been affected, he said, with an oath and a sneer, 'It has not touched *me* yet.' But soon after, God's Spirit did touch him.

"It was one Sabbath night in the beginning of August. He had ordered his children that day to go to school at the Popish chapel. Their mother, however, unknown to him, had sent them to the Presbyterian school. When they came home, learning somehow that such had been the case, he cursed and raged and threatened; and thus the Sabbath evening was spent.

"So angry was he with his wife that he vowed he would not occupy the same room with her, and went and lay down on the kitchen floor. During the night he awoke, and felt himself trembling from head to foot. He tried to rise, but could not—his side seemed benumbed. He attempted *now* to speak to his wife, but his tongue refused to move. And so he lay, trembling and praying, all night on the floor.

"In the morning he found himself able to rise and speak, and when he got up, he said to his wife and children, 'With God's help, from this time forward, I will lead a new life.'

"During the day he went to the priest. He was greatly affrighted by what had occurred, but ignorant of what he should do, and so he went to the priest for advice. But from him he got no comfort. Some of the converts, meeting him, advised him to go home and pray. He did so, and from that time began to attend our prayer-meetings, though once or twice after he went to the chapel. For the next five or six weeks his mind was in this doubting, anxious, inquiring, prayerful state, seeking rest but finding none.

"At last God fulfilled to him the promise, 'Then shall ye know, if ye follow on to know the Lord.' The truth was made manifest to his conscience. He saw himself to be a sinner, and Jesus to be the one Mediator; and his weary soul found rest in Christ. To use his own words, he 'gave himself up, soul and body, to Jesus, and trusted Him with all.'

"Since that time he has continued steadfast. No more has he gone and no more, he says will he go to the chapel, but regularly attends the Presbyterian church prayer-meetings. Every night he gets his children to read the Bible aloud, and he conducts family worship. He has a prayer-meeting in his house, in which he sometimes takes a part, pouring out his thanks and wishes and wants of God in language very homely, but very expressive. Often in his travels through the country, gathering rags, does he meet with cursing and reproach. 'You deserve to be hunted out of the country for turning,' said a Romanist to him one day. 'It was not I that turned,' was his reply; 'it was Christ that turned me, or I never would of myself.'

"As far as human eye can see, he is now a meek and lowly follower of the Lord Jesus."

Taught by a Tombstone.—The following statement is communicated by the Rev. H. P. Charleton, County Donegal:—"The circumstances which led to the conversion of a Roman Catholic, a small farmer, residing three or four miles from Londonderry, are somewhat remarkable. Some months previous to the 'revival' reaching the neighbourhood where he resides he was earning a livelihood in England. His attention had been attracted by a small house on the wayside, overgrown with ivy, and approached by a gate. He seems to have been curious as to the use to which the building was put —whether it was inhabited or not. One evening he paused in his walk and looked over the gate, when his eye fell on a tombstone bearing a rude inscription in verse, the purport of which was that those who die out of Christ must perish everlastingly. The rude and simple verses sent the arrow of conviction to his heart. For months a wakened conscience kept him uneasy. He returned to Ireland. About June 1859, a wave of the sea of grace then rising in our land swept over the neighbourhood where our convert then resided, and where he is still residing. One day he was at his devotions, and, I believe, entreating God to have mercy on him, when he was seized by one of those swoons so peculiar and so common during the season of revival. This seems to have been the turning point in his life. He has abandoned the communion of Rome—is regular in his attendance on the Presbyterian church of Burt, and on each Sabbath evening renders his aid in conducting a prayer-meeting in a hamlet in the neighbourhood of his residence. His prayers are very earnest, and remarkably scriptural, and he evidences both the gift and the grace of prayer. His life is most consistent."

Such are a few cases, out of many, in which there is good reason to believe a change has been effected, not only in the religious profession, but in the entire spiritual history of those who have experienced it. In this great awakening Rome has encountered a new adversary; and although all her arts have been resorted to—too often successfully—for the purpose of arresting inquiry and stifling conviction, the power with which she has contended is too mighty to be baffled by her machinations.[1] In the liberation of so many of her unhappy votaries without the immediate intervention of any human agency, may we not see an earnest of that day of triumph, when her knell shall be rung out in the hearing of exulting Christendom, and when heaven shall re-echo to earth the shout of jubilation that shall arise over her irrevocable doom?

[1] " The priests," says the *Quarterly Review*, in an interesting and favourable article, evidently furnished by one who has had opportunities of judging from personal observation of the movement, " denounced the revival. Many advised their flocks against this ' new work of the devil,' and represented it as an alarming contagious disease. They blessed charms and bottles of holy water, and sold them to the people to prevent them from ' catching it.' We know of one priest who realised £5 in a month, and of another who made £17 in a few weeks. A poor servant lad bought a bottle for 1s., stole into his master's room while he was at prayer, and shook the bottle over his head, to prevent him from taking the ' prevailing epidemic.' "

18
The Revival and the Pathological Affections

THE pathological phenomena which at an early period were associated with the awakening recorded in the preceding pages have been the theme of much perplexed discussion. I approach this part of the subject therefore with some degree of diffidence, especially as I am convinced that nothing can be more out of place than a tone of dogmatism in dealing with a question which demands for its solution a nice acquaintance with our complex constitution and with the laws that regulate its wondrous mechanism.

In the course of the year immediately preceding that in which the outburst of religious fervour engaged universal interest at home, I had enjoyed the privilege of witnessing, to some extent, the course of that great revival by which the churches of the New World had been visited, and which has been regarded by them as one of the most memorable displays of Divine power and mercy. Especially had I remarked its noiseless character, and its entire freedom from those tumultuous agitations which have sometimes signalised the progress of kindred movements in that land. I was well aware, too, that the ablest theologians of America, warned by the experience of the past, had both by word and deed discountenanced the physical concomitants of the awakenings by which their country has been so often favoured, and that their absence on the occasion of the late effusion of the Spirit was a theme of general congratulation.

THE PATHOLOGICAL AFFECTIONS 217

Accordingly, when a numerous and influential meeting was convened for private consultation, soon after the first appearance of the revival in Belfast, I took the opportunity of referring to such experiences, especially as enforced by Dr Hodge of Princeton, than whom America can boast no greater master in Israel. Others also made similar representations.

The pathological affections that were developed at an early period in the Ulster movement, although presenting some points of resemblance, were not identical in all respects with those delineated in the narratives of the American revivals of other days. In the latter case the voluntary muscles of the system were called into violent action, as in the well-known instances in Kentucky and other places; in the former, the symptoms were those of physical debility, and of a total sinking of muscular energy often amounting to insensibility. It was felt, therefore, that the phenomena in question should be judged of according to the phase under which they actually appeared; and, as they were a new thing in our experience, a committee was appointed to inquire into their peculiar character and into the movement generally, and to report to future meetings. These meetings were held for some time, and were under the oversight of the late Rev. Dr Wilson, Professor of Sacred Literature, one of the soundest intellects in connection with any Church. I regret that no formal statement of his views on the subject was ever published, as it might have done much to guide others at an early stage in relation to a department of such exciting interest. There is no doubt, however, that our departed friend was thoroughly convinced from the beginning of the reality of the work, although he made little account of its unusual accompaniments.

In adverting to the peculiar character of those physical affections with which we are now familiar, I may here introduce an extract from a letter, lately received by the Bishop of Down and Connor, from Bishop M'Ilvaine of Ohio :—

"As to the cases of 'striking' which have appeared so often in connection with the work in Ireland, I have recently become acquainted with some singular facts. I was conversing the other day with the grandson of a very intelligent and prominent man among the early settlers of Ohio, who said, that when those accounts from Ireland were first read among his friends, they exclaimed, 'Why, that is exactly what occurred among the Scotch-Irish in Kentucky, 1804!' The older counties of Kentucky were settled from Virginia, and from a part of Virginia which was peopled by the posterity of the Scotch-Irish Presbyterians, who originally went thither from Ireland. It was that Scotch-Irish posterity that settled Kentucky—a Presbyterian people chiefly—an intelligent, hardy, industrious, brave, and quiet set of people. About the year 1804 there occurred a great revival among them, spreading over several counties, under the preaching of certain faithful men. They met by thousands in the forests for worship—the few houses of worship being too small and scattered. The revival was followed by very permanent and marked spiritual blessings. It left its impress in the very decided Christian character of its subjects. The grandfather of my informant was one of them. Afterwards he moved to Ohio, and his son was Governor of Ohio.

"The character of the people was precisely that from which you would least expect mere excitement. They were the very ones to suspect and resist all attempts to produce excitement. But among those Scotch-Irish

THE PATHOLOGICAL AFFECTIONS

strangely appeared precisely such cases of striking as the same sort of people, in the very region whence their fathers came, have been now exhibiting. Infidels and scoffers went to see and ridicule the work, and instantly, without conscious preparatory states of mind, were stricken down. All the phases mentioned in Ireland took place in Kentucky, except that I cannot say anything of the visions (a peculiarity in which I see nothing of importance). These strikings were preached against, and not sought to be promoted; the temperament of the people was averse to them, and still they appeared; and, what is very remarkable, since the days of Jonathan Edwards, and the great revival in New England in his day (1735 and 1740), such manifestations have not appeared among any other people. We have heard of bodily effects of various kinds among some very ignorant, disorderly sects in our frontier settlements; but they were not connected with gospel truth, and were directly sought and promoted as religion, and were ludicrous as well as strange. These curious coincidents in regard to a people who have been among the very best of our populations, I mention only as matter of fact."

The first and general view taken of the phenomena in question by the religious portion of the public was that, on whatever theory they might be accounted for, it was a great thing if, under any circumstances, men were awakened from the almost universal death-sleep into which they had fallen. That might be real which was not beneficial; and as in the growth of a plant there is a development of much which does not effloresce in blossom or ripen into fruit, why might there not be certain associated developments even in connection with religion, the highest work of God, which, though not of the nature of true godliness, have yet some relation to its production ? So reasoned the calmest and least excitable among us. Nor did they think it wonderful that persons who had been unfamiliar with the experiences of the higher life, and wholly untrained in spiritual things, when suddenly overborne by Divine influence, should find an outlet for the expression of their soul agony through other than the usual, and, as we say, legitimate channels ; and that, tossed upon the stormy billows, they should not well know how to carry themselves, and drift almost uncontrollably away. Better, surely, to breast the roaring surge on the live ocean, and speed on before the favouring gale, than lie becalmed and motionless amid the stagnation and putridity of the waveless sea of death.

From the beginning, too, as has once and again been indicated in this narrative, there was a general impression that the strange excitement by which, in almost every district, this great impulsive movement was ushered in, might have a profound moral significance. So insensate are the generality of men, that nothing can exceed their indisposition to realise the spiritual and invisible ; and why should not the quickening Spirit, through the medium of strange and startling things on earth, arouse the dormant intellect to the contemplation of the far stranger things in heaven ? Might not these unwonted incidents, in the case of a people naturally impassive, who, although familiar with the gospel scheme, had practically rejected it, be regarded as an alarm-cry from eternity of awful import—a trumpet-call to arouse the sleepers from their fatal slumber ? Were they not at least entitled to rank with those inscrutable visitations of disease and famine which have proved the divinely-commissioned messengers of mercy as well as judgment, by which men have often been arrested in

THE PATHOLOGICAL AFFECTIONS

their unconcern, and led to flee from the wrath to come?

Whatever may be the solution of these visitations, there is no doubt that by their suddenness they surprised and awed the minds of the community. A sensible and solemn dread, not unmixed with superstition, fell even upon the most hardened and abandoned, when, on this side and on that, so many were visibly passing through such agonised experiences; and those who before had mocked were seized with mortal terror, like criminals whose hour had come. No wonder that profanity and profligacy cowered in their awful presence, and looked reverently on, when such tempest-heavings of emotion were almost rending asunder the mortal tabernacle. And when the hurricane had spent its force, and the scene of such wild commotion was lighted up by the calm sunshine of an untroubled heaven; when one and another, who had lived long years in utter disregard of all that an immortal being should most diligently seek to realise, had, after having being bowed down like a bulrush, risen up to newness of life, the entire bent of mind and character transformed, and the chambers of imagery, so dark before, irradiated as by a celestial brightness; and when the witnesses were the everyday acquaintances, and in many cases the intimate connections, of those who had experienced the marvellous transition,—how could it be otherwise than that the new-born wonder of the moment should give place to the intelligent and admiring contemplation of the astounding moral revolutions that were being wrought? A single transmutation of this description, with its attendant circumstances, was a no less convincing attestation to the presence of a Divine agency than if one had risen from the dead,—it brought near to every one, and almost forced upon the senses of the beholder, the dread realities of the world to come.

Such were the impressions, for the most part, produced on serious men by the peculiar character of the religious movement and its accessories in the North of Ireland. That the latter were always wisely treated it would be contrary to evidence and experience to assert, for there were those who seemed in every case to regard them as due to a direct influence of the Spirit of God. Had such views prevailed extensively, it is not difficult to say what excesses would have been committed, and what occasion would have been given to the adversary to speak reproachfully. It was well for Ulster and for religion that throughout the country there was a body of educated and enlightened ministers, who from the outset set themselves to repress extravagance and excess, and to eliminate from the scenes they witnessed those spiritual influences which were so manifestly at work, though frequently commingling with baser elements. The disorders that have taken place in some quarters are largely to be attributed either to the lukewarmness of those who might have been expected to direct the movement, or the too ardent temperament of others who allowed themselves to be borne along, irrespective of the course it took, upon every outflow of the tide of excited feeling, or to the peculiar position of a third class, who, though favourably affected to the new state of things, were not in circumstances to render much efficient service in guiding and directing it.

It has been stated in an early part of this volume that in the neighbourhood of Connor, where a gracious work had been in progress for eighteen months before public attention was concentrated upon it, there were no violent agitations such as were elsewhere subsequently witnessed.

Hundreds were led to serious consideration, and passed through a spiritual crisis, under the silent operation of the truth ; nor were there any outcries or prostrations in all the district. That apprehension of things spiritual arises from Divine illumination, has nothing in it which of necessity violently deranges the bodily organism, although instances are on record in the Bible, in which gracious affections would seem to have been accompanied by much physical depression ; nor is there anything in the Word of God to countenance the idea that "bodily exercise" of this description must be the legitimate effect of religious feeling. We do not find such results attendant on the personal ministry of our Lord and His apostles—not even on that solemn day when the awful truth flashed on the bewildered and confounded listeners that He whom they had crucified was both Lord and Christ. Doubtless, the depths of moral feeling were then profoundly stirred ; and conscience, with its self-reproaches, was doing its proper work, when from that mighty multitude, "pricked to the heart," there arose the agonised and imploring cry,—"Men and brethren, what shall we do ?"

Nor is there any stress laid in the Scriptures on such feelings as are excited through the medium of the imagination. This faculty, like every other, has an almost boundless field presented to it, over which to expatiate in the system of revealed truth. As on a seraph's wing it may soar afar into the regions of ethereal light and purity, and take its stand upon the sapphire pavement of the city of the great King. At one time it may scan the heavenly hierarchy, as they attend the "throne and equipage of God's almightiness," or cast their crowns before that radiant form once marred more than any, now clothed with unearthly splendour. At another it may take a downward plunge, and hold converse with spirits in the doleful shades, recoiling at the imagery with which it has itself invested the realms of the outer darkness. From such materials it may conjure up many a wondrous spectacle; now rapt as in Elysian bowers, now racked as in intolerable and endless torment. But while the imagination has its legitimate province in relation to the things of God, there is danger that it may rest on what is merely figurative, to the comparative neglect of the solid and stable truth which figure is intended to convey. And " when an affection," as Edwards has it, " arises from the imagination, and is built upon it as its foundation, instead of a spiritual illumination or discovery, then is the affection, however elevated, worthless and vain. . . . . . When the Spirit of God is poured out to begin a glorious work, then the old serpent, as fast as possible, and by all means, introduces this bastard religion, which has from time to time brought all things into confusion. . . . . . The imagination or fantasy seems to be that wherein are formed all those delusions of Satan which those are carried away with who are under the influence of false religion and counterfeit graces and affections. There is the devil's grand lurking-place, the very nest of foul and delusive spirits."

It is further to be borne in mind that bodily agitations, visions, and trances, in their varied modifications, have been associated in their history, not only with genuine revivals, but with kindred excitements, in all countries and ages. " That they are all alike attributable to the same cause," says Dr Hodge, " is probable because they arise under the same circumstances, are propagated by the same means, and cured by the same treatment. They arise in seasons of great, and especially of general excitement; they, in a great majority of cases, affect the ignorant rather than the enlightened, those in whom the imagination predominates over the reason, and especially those who are of a nervous temperament, rather than those of an opposite character. These affections all propagate themselves by a kind of infection. This circumstance is characteristic of the whole class of nervous diseases. Physicians enumerate among the causes of epilepsy, 'seeing a person in convulsions.' This fact was so well known that the Romans made a law, that if any one should be seized with epilepsy during the meeting of the comitia, the assembly should be dissolved. This disease occurred so frequently in those exciting meetings, and was propagated so rapidly, that it was called the *morbus comitialis*. . . . . . Sometimes such affections become epidemic, spreading over whole provinces. In the fifteenth century a violent nervous disease, attended with convulsions and other analogous symptoms, extended over a great part of Germany, especially affecting the inmates of the convents. In the next century something of the same kind prevailed extensively in the South of France. These affections were then regarded as the result of demoniacal possessions and, in some instances, multitudes of poor creatures were put to death as demoniacs."

It is a characteristic circumstance respecting the physical affections thus referred to, that they have rarely appeared, or at least they have not long continued, when not approved or encouraged. Thus, says Hodge, "in Northampton, where Edwards rejoiced over them, they were abundant; in Boston, where they were regarded as 'blemishes,' they had nothing of them. In Sutton, Massachusetts, they were 'cautiously guarded against,' and consequently never appeared, except among strangers from other congregations. Only one or two cases occurred in Elizabethtown, under President Dickinson, who considered them as 'irregular heats,' and those few were speedily regulated. There was nothing of the kind at Freehold, where William Tennent set his face against all such manifestations of enthusiasm. On the other hand, they followed Davenport and other fanatical preachers almost wherever they went. In Scotland they were less encouraged than they were here, and consequently prevailed less. In England, where Wesley regarded them as certainly from God, they were fearful, both as to their frequency and violence. A physician, already quoted, says, 'Restraint often prevents a paroxysm. For example, persons always attacked by this affection in churches where it is encouraged, will be perfectly calm in churches where it is discouraged, however affecting may be the service, and however great the mental excitement.' " [1]

I have thought it right to introduce these striking testimonies from one who, though himself one of the most eminent and experienced of theologians, is not less remarkable for his saintly grace and for his surpassing tenderness. Often, as I am assured, when he is addressing his students at those Sabbath conferences in which they meet together for edification as well as instruction, the venerable divine of Princeton is overcome by deep emotion, and his overflowing heart finds vent in tears. It is from no want of genuine sympathy, therefore, either with the distress of awakened or the joy of delivered souls, that he records such a decided judgment on the subject of those physical developments which in his own country have been the occasion of much anxious consideration.

As showing the strange and unreliable character of

[1] Hist. p. 78.

such affections elsewhere, I may here introduce a brief statement with reference to their appearance among the Camisards of France, as supplied by Herzog in his "Encyclopædia," p. 539 (Edinburgh edition)—

"In 1688 many persons in Dauphiné, mostly females, commenced, in half-sleeping, half-waking ecstatics, to exhort people to repentance and faith, speaking fluently and correctly, though in common life theirs was a provincial brogue. In these exhortations they showed an extensive acquaintance with the Bible, wanting to them when awake. Before long, children began to fall down during the meetings of the Reformed, who would warn them of traitors and enemies, that proved to be really at hand. The number of prophets increased rapidly— all Dauphiné and Languedoc were full of them. Thus the Reformed were strengthened, but the fire of persecution also grew in the same degree. When these real supernatural manifestations gradually began to fail, impure, fictitious, and even demoniac prophecies took their place, especially as the persecution, too, assumed so malignant a character."

On the medical aspects of the question under consideration I shall not largely enter. It is right to state, however, that the recognised organs of the faculty in London and Edinburgh substantially regard the physiological features of this movement as, if not decidedly hysterical, yet of the nature of "irregular hysteria"— a morbid condition produced by some emotion seeking for itself an outlet denied through its natural channels of activity—the pent-up force producing a paroxysmal fit proportionate in severity and duration to the original strength of the feeling, or to the exhaustion resulting from efforts to repress it, the movements occurring in no fixed order, so that the presence or absence of "globus" (the ball in the throat), is not conclusive with regard to its existence.[1].

In medical disquisitions, such as I am adverting to, the connection between our emotive nature and its physical manifestations occupies a leading place. There are, according to the physiologists, in the human system, three grand centres of nervous influence. In the higher region there is the brain, the seat of thought; in the inferior, the sensorium (as it is popularly named), the seat of feeling; whence downward extends the spinal chord, the source of motion; and as each of the changes, whether in the superior or inferior organs, disengages " force," it is averred that we have in this a solution of the effects of strong emotion on our corporeal frame.

Thus, then, according to physiology, as expounded by its ablest investigators, such as Drs Carpenter and Carter, emotive force will manifest itself in outward effect, now operating downwards, if unduly excited, on the automatic nerves, in which case its action will be seen on the physical energies; now operating upwards on the brain, and influencing reason, will, and conscience; or, again, taking both an upward and downward direction at the same moment, when a complex result may be evolved. The phenomena produced, in so far as they are the effect of action on the sensorium, are regarded as manifestations of a disordered state of the nervous system, to which the general name hysteria is applied, though under that designation many anomalous cases are included, not witnessed by the physician in his ordinary practice, but sufficiently analogous to others that are familiar, as to warrant their being referred to a common cause—namely, the excitation of those emotions which, when in their normal state, are regulated

[1] See *Journal of Psychological Medicine* for January 1860.

and controlled by the higher faculties. All nervous affections, we are further assured, have an extraordinary power of self-propagation, either by sympathy or by that " expectant attention " which, in periods of great excitement, and even in some of the more alarming epidemics, such as cholera, operates frequently as a predisposing cause. And for illustrations in abundance, we are referred to such works as that of Hecker on the Epidemics of the Middle Ages, in which, among other similar instances, he gives a full account of the French *convulsionnaires*, and of the enthusiasts who frequented the tomb of the Abbé Paris, in the beginning of the last century.

Medical science thus claiming to be heard on one leading department of the question, why should any be jealous of its testimony ? To refuse or undervalue it, were wilfully to close our eyes in a case into every phase of which we are required, by a regard to the high interests involved, so institute a most sifting scrutiny. Some may seek to arrest inquiry by the assertion of miraculous intervention ; but such a course is alien to the genius of Protestant Christianity. If certain of the accompaniments of the revival can be accounted for on natural principles, let us by all means so dispose of them. To call in the aid of the supernatural for the solution of any ordinary phenomemon were a serious error, alike in logic and theology.

Is it possible, however, even with the aids of science in its present state of advancement, to account for all the pathological phenomena by any purely physical theory ? And even if it were, would this remove them from under Divine superintendence and control ? May not every one of them be capable of solution by the known laws that link together our mental and corporeal organisms, and yet be charged with a most important and specific spiritual mission? Does not the Moral Governor rule by law in everything, and yet who will deny His ever-present agency amid the constancy and uniformity of nature? Granting, therefore, that a satisfactory explanation on physiological principles could be given of the phenomena under review, that would not sever the connection between these manifestations and the finger of God in them. Some such concessions, it is gratifying to find, are made by the medical authorities themselves. Thus the *Edinburgh Medical Journal* for January writes—" The anti-revivalists are quite in error if they imagine that when they have proved the 'cases' to be hysterical, they have disposed of the whole case. It is quite possible that even in these instances salutary impressions may co-exist with the ebullitions of emotional feeling, and the symptoms of actual disease." While the reviewer in Dr Winslow's *Journal of Psychological Medicine* introduces the element of " demoniac agency " as one of the perverting causes in a time of " visitation."

May we not, then, arrive at a solution of both the spiritual and the physical phenomena that will not traverse any of the known laws of our constitution? I do not know that we have sufficient data, or that it lies within the range of our knowledge, fully to solve this question. Nor is it, perhaps, for practical purposes needful that we should do more than disentangle the higher process from that which has no necessary connection with it, discountenancing all tendency to rest in anything but what is spiritual as an evidence of a saving change. At the same time, it is desirable that we should reduce the cases, of whatever description, under their proper heads; and these, I humbly submit, are the three following:—

THE PATHOLOGICAL AFFECTIONS

I. Those in which the bodily effects are traceable to *strongly excited mental action*. Under this class will fall to be ranked by far the greater number ordinarily witnessed. The mental action, I am persuaded, as a general rule, is the immediate and invariable antecedent of the bodily affection. It cannot for a moment be supposed that the phenomena in question demand a specific theory, as though a new mode of the operation of the Divine Spirit directly upon our corporeal organism, and irrespective of the laws of mind, had been introduced among us. I am aware that here and there a few cases are reported, and some in the preceding pages, in which the parties affected are represented by themselves as wholly unconscious of any mental impression anterior to the physical prostration. But such representations are too loosely made to be of much real value. Who does not know that there are states of consciousness that vanish almost as soon as they arise, and leave no trace behind ? Especially when violent emotion ensues, how difficult for the subject of it to analyse or even to remember the antecedent operation of the intellect ? May not a dominant idea produce its appropriate effects, without leaving any distinct impression on the mental tablet, whether we adopt the theory that there are mental states of which we have no consciousness, or that in certain cases the mind, though conscious of its own operations, gives them too little attention to imprint them on the memory ?

I am aware also that there are some sudden and characteristic cases of persons being "stricken" in their own houses, on the road, or in the field ; and some more peculiar still, in which resistance to the work has shown itself by mocking and deriding it ; and the popular opinion in regard to these is that they came without any premonition from within. But though the state of mind in such cases may have appeared to an onlooker to be one only of impervious hostility to the work, may it not be as readily accounted for by the attempt to drown conviction and stifle conscience, under the transparent guise of an unseemly and unnatural levity?

II. There are other cases of which the only satisfactory solution that can be given is that they are attributable to *the principle of sympathy*. I need not here descant on the peculiar character or extensive influence of this principle, as one of most important application for good or evil. Let me rather supply a case in illustration of its influence in a time of religious excitement in America, as narrated by the Rev. Dr Archibald Alexander of Princeton, in his admirable volume " On Religious Experience ; " showing sufficiently that spiritual convictions are not necessary to create physical manifestations, and that, in a season of awakening, there may be those who are even violently agitated, whose consciences give all the while no evidence of being quickened by a higher agency. He justly observes that ministers cannot prevent the impressions which arise mainly from sympathy ; neither should they attempt it ; but when they are about to gather the wheat into the garner, they should faithfully winnow the heap.

" Being in a part of the country where I was known face to face to scarcely any one, and hearing that there was a great meeting in the neighbourhood, and a good work in progress, I determined to attend. The sermon had commenced before I arrived, and the house was so crowded that I could not approach near to the pulpit, but sat down in a kind of shed connected with the main building, where I could see and hear the preacher. His sermon was really striking and impressive, and in lan-

THE PATHOLOGICAL AFFECTIONS 233

guage and method far above the common rule of extempore discourses. The people were generally attentive, and, so far as I could observe, many were tenderly affected, excepting that, in the extreme part of the house where I sat, some old tobacco-planters kept up a continual conversation, in a low tone, about tobacco-plants, seasons, &c. When the preacher came to the application of his discourse, he became exceedingly vehement and boisterous, and I could hear some sounds in the centre of the house which indicated strong emotion. At length a female voice was heard in a piercing cry, which thrilled through me, and affected the whole audience. It was succeeded by a low, murmuring sound from the middle of the house; but in a few seconds one and another rose in different parts of the house, under extreme and visible agitation. Casting off bonnets and caps, and raising their folded hands, they shouted to the utmost extent of their voice; and in a few seconds more the whole audience was agitated, as a forest when shaken by a mighty wind.

"The sympathetic wave, commencing in the centre, extended to the extremities, and at length it reached our corner, and I felt the conscious effort of resistance as necessary as if I had been exposed to the violence of a storm. I saw few persons throughout the whole house who escaped the prevailing influence; even careless boys seemed to be arrested, and to join in the general outcry. But what astonished me most of all was, that the old tobacco-planters whom I have mentioned, and who, I am persuaded, had not heard one word of the sermon, were violently agitated. Every muscle of their brawny faces appeared to be in tremulous motion, and the big tears chased one another down their wrinkled cheeks. There I saw the power of sympathy. The feeling was real, and propagated from person to person by the mere sounds which were uttered—for many of the audience had not paid any attention to what was said—but nearly all partook of the agitation. The feelings expressed were different, as when the foundation of the second temple was laid; for while some uttered the cry of poignant anguish, others shouted in the accents of joy and triumph. The speaker's voice was soon silenced, and he sat down and gazed on the scene with a complacent smile.

"When this tumult had lasted a few minutes, another preacher, as I suppose he was, also sat on the pulpit steps, with his handkerchief spread over his head, and began to sing a soothing, and yet lively tune, and was quickly joined by some strong female voices near him; and in less than two minutes the storm was hushed, and there was a great calm. It was like pouring oil on the troubled waters. I experienced the most sensible relief to my own feelings from the appropriate music, for I could not hear the words sung; but I could not have supposed that anything could so quickly allay such a storm;— and all seemed to enjoy the tranquillity which succeeded. The dishevelled hair was put in order, the bonnets, &c., gathered up, and the irregularities of the dress adjusted, and no one seemed conscious of any impropriety. Indeed, there is a peculiar luxury in such excitements, especially when tears are shed copiously—which was the case here. But I attended another meeting in another place, where there had been a remarkable excitement, but the tide was far on the ebb; and although we had vociferation and outcrying of a stunning kind, I did not hear one sound indicative of real feeling, and I do not think that one tear was shed during the meeting."

THE PATHOLOGICAL AFFECTIONS 235

III. There is a third class of cases, which, either in whole or in part, may be ascribed to *the operation of nervous disease.* That such a disease, call it by what name we may, and by whatever means originated and propagated, has in most places been running parallel with the spiritual movement, does not admit of question. To be aware of its existence is the first step in the process towards its proper treatment. That it may be either checked or stimulated, past experience, especially in the case of the American awakenings, has sufficiently established. It requires, no doubt, a measure of discrimination and decision to deal aright with such manifestations, which, wherever they exist, are generally encouraged by the common people, who take pleasure in all strong excitement. Still, it is all-important, for the sake of those who are the subjects of them, as well as for the character and credit of the work with which they may be accidently associated, that in so far as they are merely corporeal, they be kept in their own proper place of relative insignificance.

Judging by the past amongst ourselves, there is a tendency, prevailing however but to a limited extent, to cultivate the "prostrations," as though they were the starting-point in the process of conversion. How necessary, therefore, that enlightened views upon the subject should be diffused, and that the public mind should be drawn off from these at best incidental accompaniments of the work of God! "The apology made in Corinth," says Dr Hodge, speaking of similar affections, "for the disorders which Paul condemned, was precisely the same as that urged in defence of these bodily agitations. 'We ought not to resist the Spirit of God,' said the Corinthians, and so said all those who encouraged these convulsions. Paul's answer was, that no influence which comes from God destroys our self-control. ' The spirits of the prophets are subject to the prophets.' Even in the case of direct inspiration and revelation, the mode of communication was in harmony with our rational nature, and left our powers under the control of reason and the will. The man, therefore, who felt the divine affection, had no right to give way to it under circumstances which would produce noise and confusion."

In the case of those who have been physically affected, whether at the period of the spiritual change or subsequently, nothing surely can be more inconsiderate or reprehensible than to subject them to the likelihood of a repetition of the affection, which, as often as it is reproduced, tends to exhaust the frame and to induce permanent disease. It is most distressing to hear of young females being fifty, a hundred, and, as in one case of which I am advised, two hundred times " stricken." Wherever there is a predisposition to this tendency, it were alike a duty and a kindness to isolate the individual as much as possible from all exciting causes ; to resist, as an intrusion, the presence of every curious visitor ; and to draw off the mind from its own exercises by some suitable occupation. This course has been followed in many instances, and with the happiest effect.

Account as we may, however, for the complex phenomena which have presented themselves in connection with the movement under consideration, one thing is certain, that no possible combination of mental or material elements could leave behind it, irrespective of a higher agency, the residuum of renewed souls. With the vast majority of the " affected," the secret of the matter was that one over-mastering sentiment took hold of them, and carried them away, sometimes they knew not whither. It was not so much a sense of danger as a

THE PATHOLOGICAL AFFECTIONS 237

sense of sin that crushed them down,—an apprehension of the awful holiness of God, and a more than ordinary realisation of the evil of offending Him. And what if, before the astounding disclosures then opened up in all their terrible distinctness, any should have given way— the sympathetic feeling intensifying the impression— till, all unused to restrain the natural outflow of emotion, they should break forth in the wild cry of horror and despair ? Was it a time to look on with censorious eye, when the heavens were rending and the earth was shaking at the presence of the Lord ? And though we may congratulate the district or the community in which a wide-spread spiritual interest has been awakened in the absence of tumultuous excitement ; yet shall we refuse to recognise the presence and the power of the Eternal, even although some strange things should have happened, and here and there a few should have been disordered by unhealthy stimulants and injudicious treatment ? Is not the process of conversion, under any circumstances, the result of a superhuman agency ? and why should it be thought extraordinary if, when a whole community is stirred, there should be a proportionate increase in its abnormal accompaniments ?

I shall only add, with reference to the affections so frequently referred to, that there is no ground to believe that they have conducted those who were the subjects of them along a higher pathway than has been trodden by others in whom the momentous change was wrought without any experience of them ; while in many cases they have developed some peculiarity of temperament or character which has called forth, on behalf of the " affected," a more than ordinary solicitude on the part of such as have been interested in their spiritual progress.

With reference to the cases of dumbness and the like,

which were for a time an occasion of much stupid wonder to many, I cannot better express the view entertained of them by all who are intelligently informed, than by quoting the following passage from the able and most seasonable paper presented by my excellent friend, Dr M'Cosh, to the Annual Conference of the Evangelical Alliance at its meeting in Belfast in September last :—

"From an organism weakened by repeated excitement, proceed cases of blindness and dumbness, and of persons who can bring on sleep at a particular time, and awake at an appointed hour. I have found in a vast number of cases that the deafness and blindness have appeared, not in persons who have been struck the first time with a conviction of sin, but in persons who have been struck a number of times. It is a warning, given in God's natural providence, that in that particular district the bodily excitement is being carried too far, and is in danger of overriding and oppressing the spiritual work. All such persons should be put under the care of a kind Christian physician ; they should be encouraged to pray that their bodily weakness may be relieved as speedily as possible ; and to seek to come under the influence of faith and confidence and love, which, instead of weakening the body, have a tendency to soothe and strengthen the frame. As to the sleeping cases, every one who has studied the subject knows that mesmerism is full of them. A trained traveller can fall asleep when he pleases, and rise at any hour he fixes ; and people in a mesmeric state can anticipate and regulate their mesmeric slumbers. If there be any persons so preposterously foolish—I had almost said blasphemous—as to ascribe such cases to the Spirit of God, I would remind them that the Hindoos can produce far more wonderful cases than those in Ireland ; for, in India, individuals who have acquired this mesmeric power allow themselves to be buried for days, and tell beforehand the precise time when they are to awake, and their friends are to open the ground to allow them to rise. When such cases appear, Christians should by all means discourage them. They were just beginning in a village with which I am acquainted, when a Christian physician, who had been the main earthly leader of the movement in the district, reasoned with the people, and they immediately disappeared. Great mischief arises from such persons being visited by neighbours and strangers, as if they were objects of admiration, whereas they are rather objects for our commiseration and our prayers. I have often seen that the people who go wondering after such cases are of all persons the least likely to wish to become partakers of the spiritual work. Nothing, in my humble opinion, is so much fitted to grieve the Spirit, as to find persons gazing at the weakness of man, as if it were the power of God. The only thoroughly conceited converts I have seen in this movement, are those who have got into such a state of physical weakness that they see visions and predict events. The predictions, I may remark, have all the characteristic marks of *clairvoyance*, which has so often been exposed. I may add, that while cases of this description have hitherto been very few, yet we have already evidence that if encouragement were given, especially of a pecuniary kind, deception is ready to appear, and Satan would triumph."

Let me here also introduce a statement illustrative of the good effects that are sure to follow when such cases as those referred to are judiciously treated. The narrator is the Rev. Alexander Field, of Dervock, a highly-intelligent young minister of the Presbyterian

Church. It will be seen from the introductory sentences that he warmly entered into the movement, and that the results in his congregation were most encouraging:—

"It is unnecessary for me to enter into a minute detail of the blessed movement as it came under my notice. It was distinguished here by the prostrations and those other features that characterised it elsewhere, with which you and the public are so familiar. Suffice it to say, that great good has been its result in this locality and the surrounding district. I am happy to say that the *trance cases*, which were so prevalent in some quarters, were not numerous within my bounds; I believe there were only three such cases. Two of these came particularly under my cognisance, and I shall briefly inform you how I dealt with them.

"In the first case I was specially sent for by the girl herself to see her fall into the trance state. She had been 'ill' on the previous night, and had been told, she said, among other revelations from the spiritual world, that she was to be in the same condition three times more, and on the following evening at a certain hour. I was with her at the appointed time, being anxious to see a case of the kind, and to try whether I could do anything in the way of prevention. There was no watch nor clock in the house, and I forbade all reference to time by the inmates. However, at the predicted hour, she became strangely ill. I took her outside, thinking that the fresh air might remove the affection, and kept up a brisk conversation, eliciting replies to my questions, that thus I might, if possible, ward off the threatened dumbness. I succeeded for some time, but at length she signified her inability to speak. I then, in a determined but kind manner, told her that I believed she could speak, if she chose to make the effort; and reminded her that she had read of Jesus when on earth always opening the mouth, never of making people dumb, and that He was the 'same Jesus' now that He was in heaven; and also that it was her duty to glorify God by exercising the faculty of speech with which He had blessed her. This had the desired effect, and she spoke, and continued to speak during the remainder of the evening. I acted in a similar manner in reference to her eyes, which she had persisted in keeping shut; and at last I left her quite well, possessing the power of all her faculties. She never afterwards had a return of the attack; and so the predictions of the previous night came not to pass.

"The second case was that of a young woman, not then connected with my congregation. I was going my rounds, visiting those of my flock who had been 'stricken' when I was met on the road by her mother, who earnestly solicited me to go into her house and see her, stating that she was then in the trance state, and had intimated that her state was to last for seventeen hours. I went with her to please her, not expecting that I would be of any service—my experience in the former case not warranting me to conclude that I could bring a person *out* of the trance state, but only that I might be able to *prevent* her falling *into* it. On entering the house I found her daughter lying on a bed, and apparently unconscious, deaf, dumb, and blind. I engaged in devotional exercises, and then proceeded to deal with her as in the other case, firmly and kindly telling her to open her eyes and to speak, and expressing my conviction that she could do so, if she chose to make the effort. This not having any effect, I then opened her hands, which were clenched like a person's in epilepsy, and lifted up her eyelids. Gradually consciousness returned, and she evidently both saw and heard me. I next got her mouth opened, and, on looking in, observed that her tongue was tucked back so that she could not speak, but by means of water and the friction of her own finger her tongue was unloosed, and the low voice of prayer announced that her power of speech was regained. After a little, she arose from her bed, dressed, and accompanied me to the house, a little way off, whither I was proceeding when her mother met me. The recovery was complete. For eight weeks previous she had been seldom out of these trances; her health was much impaired; her physician had been tried in vain; and her parents had been exceedingly distressed; but since that day there has been no return of the state, and her bodily health has been completely restored. I leave you to draw your own conclusion from these cases. My own theory was, that somehow or other her will had become dormant, and imagination and desire had got control of the mental system. In my treatment my object was to reinvest the will with its proper authority, in the hope that, having once regained its place, it would retain it; and in this I was not disappointed. The effort of the party to resist the disposition to the trance state so strengthened the power of the will that neither imagination nor desire could afterwards overcome it.

" There were no more cases of this kind within my bounds after these two. My success in treating them brought them rather into disrepute, and consequently they ceased."

The explanation given by the Rev. E. Stopford, Archdeacon of Meath, of such cases is worthy of being introduced here:—

" The dumbness is perfectly accounted for by the hysteric action of the nerves of the throat. The blindness may be accounted for either on the same ground or by hysteric action extending to that part of the sensorium which receives the nerves of sight. The visions and revelations are due to hysterical suppression of the powers of will and reason, leaving the operation of the cerebrum and sensorium as uncontrolled as in dreams. . . . . It does not seem impossible that hysteric affection of a portion of the sensorium should cause temporary deafness; but when so unusual a phenomemon becomes prevalent a knowledge of hysteria suggests another solution. . . . 'The pleasure of receiving unwonted sympathy,' says Dr Carter, 'once tasted, excites a desire for it that knows no bounds; and when the fits have become familiar occurrences, and cease to excite attention, their effect is often heightened by the designed imitation of some other disease.' . . . . If they hear of deafness in others, they will be deaf. I cannot look on this as ordinary imposture. It is the diseased moral action of hysteria. . . . . The foretelling of the duration of dumbness, &c., or the time of recovery, is easily explained. The desire does itself induce the hysteric action, and can equally determine its cessation."

The following is a somewhat amusing instance of the way in which a prophet and a sleeper were both arrested, and a real service rendered to the neighbourhood in which the scene occurred :—

In a country parish of County Down, of which a decided work of grace has been recorded in this volume, and in the bounds of his own congregation, which received so largely of the blessing, the Presbyterian minister happened one day to call at a house where several of the inmates had been awakened, taking with him two Scottish brethren, who were anxious to be informed, by personal observation, of the real character of the work. Scarcely had they been seated, when two country-looking young men, one of whom was only some eighteen years of age, entered the house, and without any ceremony seated themselves in the apartment. The younger immediately intimated, with much show of importance, that his comrade would fall asleep in ten minutes after, and would not awake for two hours. He was at once challenged by my friend the minister, who asked him to produce his credentials substantiating his claim to the prophetic gift. When he was dealing with the young man in question, and charging him either with being an impostor or the victim of delusion, the breast of his companion began to heave, and he closed his eyes as if to induce the approach of the wondrous sleep. The *pastor loci*, however, continued his admonition, exhorting his reluctant auditor quietly to go home, to mind his proper business, and ask forgiveness for his presumption. He reminded him that even the gift of prophecy, supposing he were endowed with it, was no evidence of grace; referring to the case of Balaam, who, though he had uttered true predictions, fell fighting against Israel, and to the protestations that, at the great day, shall be made by many who will in vain appeal, in arrest of judgment, to their having prophesied in the name of Christ. He enforced especially upon him the duty of humility as the becoming ornament of the Christian profession, rating him soundly for his unceremonious intrusion into the presence of several ministers and others to whom he was an entire stranger, and who had other things to mind than sleeping cases and their prophesiers.

The brethren who were present joined in the objurgatory strictures, and addressed themselves with great earnestness to the older visitor, as to the inutility, either

THE PATHOLOGICAL AFFECTIONS

to himself or any other, of his falling into the state announced; while my friend also remonstrated with him on the unseasonableness of such an operation in such a place, and the absurdity of imagining that any good purpose could under any circumstances be served by it. The sleeper and the seer were alike nonplussed by this unexpected reception, and left the house, but not till more than twice ten minutes had elapsed after the announcement of the " prediction." It was cause of congratulation that this, the first attempt to import the sleeping fits into the neighbourhood, was so successfully resisted, as, hearing of such things around them, the people might otherwise have fallen into like disorder and extravagance. It was the only case of the kind within the district, and the mode in which it was met and put to shame called forth an expression of unmingled satisfaction from the entire community.

I shall conclude this chapter by a statement of a case of thrilling interest, which occurred in Armagh. Two of my correspondents in that city have referred to it, and from the statements they have supplied I am enabled to present it in the fullest and most authentic form :—

There was a youth of seventeen years of age, the son of a widow, who was attending the prayer-meeting one evening, and who remained behind, along with a number more, to converse with the ministers in regard to the great concerns then pressing heavily on many souls. Restless and agitated, he rose after a short period, and left the church. He repaired in the first instance to a service in another place of worship, but soon after turned homeward. Arriving at the door, he found that the key, which had been left by his employers for himself and companions, was not to be found, and turning to the street, he met a young man of the city whom he knew to be a serious Christian, to whom he said, abruptly, "Oh, what am I to do? My heart will break; I am for ever lost!" His friend urged him to accompany him to the church. "I was there already," he replied, "but all in vain." He complied, however, with the invitation, and arriving, sat down. The auditory had all dispersed except some dozen individuals, with whom the ministers were holding earnest conversation, eliciting their doubts and difficulties, and of whom several that night were led to profess their faith in Christ, and to " go on their way rejoicing."

"We were in the act of bringing this meeting to a close," says the Rev. William Henderson, "when we were surprised and startled by words of earnest prayer from a young man in the adjoining pew, who was bowed on his knees in supplication. I shall never forget the scene that followed. For about two hours that young man continued pleading with God, and wrestling with Satan, and he ceased not till he rose a conqueror, exulting in the blood of the Lamb. It is now seven months since this occurrence, and during that period I have had frequent opportunity of observing this youth, who is engaged in business in town, and I have not yet known him to falter in his burning love to Jesus, nor to waver in the strong hope which God gave him that night. His prayer was the most wonderful one that I ever listened to. Many of his utterances are yet vividly impressed on my memory. Aided by some notes, which were hurriedly taken by a brother minister at the time, I subjoin a few of the petitions, as well as expostulations with the enemy, which fell from his lips:—

" . . . . 'Satan, thou enemy of my soul, begone!— thou deceiver of the world, leave me! Come not near me, Satan, for Jesus is here! O Jesus, save me! Thou didst smite Saul of Tarsus, the persecutor of Thy Church, and Thou hast smitten me, an enemy of Thy cross, an enemy of Thy Bible, an enemy of Thy Sabbath, an enemy of mankind. O Jesus, heal my wounded heart! Jesus Christ, the Righteous One, save my soul! Satan, thou father of lies, I have served thee long. I have been a subject of thy kingdom; but now thy chains are breaking. Keep back, Satan! . . . O eternal Son of God, have mercy! O Spirit of the living God, draw near to me! . . . O Jesus! Thou didst come to Bethlehem's manger—Thou didst come to Gethsemane's garden—Thou didst come to Calvary's cross—Thou didst love poor sinners. . . . O thou Saviour of the lost, save *me!* Thou hast arrested me in the broad road which leads down to hell. I see my companions hurrying downward. Oh, have mercy on my poor soul! I see my sin as a great mountain,—wash it away! O Spirit, Thou hast smitten, but, Jesus, do Thou heal the wound! My sins are like a thick, dark, dismal cloud,—oh, shine over it and take it away! . . . Oh, human nature, sinful, vile, polluted, hell-deserving! Holy Spirit, I thank Thee for Thy glorious work. . . . O Saviour, Thou art here. I see Thy face. It is shining, it is radiant—it is radiant like the sun, yea, like millions of suns. Little wonder that Satan is confounded before Thee! . . . Jesus, Thou didst say to the raging sea, " Peace, be still," and there was a great calm. Let it be so here! . . . Thou hast taken me away from my past life—it is all a blank, it is a black catalogue of sin. . . . . O Saviour—*the* Saviour—*the* Saviour, help me! Oh, let Thy glory be advanced in this smitten soul! . . . Oh for faith! Faith is the wanting grace. . . . Oh, the conflict is sore! . . . O Jesus, gather in all my wandering thoughts, and cluster them on Thy cross, and take and purify them from sin! ... Satan, it is hard to baffle thee. Oh, come not near this poor, naked, wounded soul! Say not there is no mercy! Ah! there is mercy for the chief of sinners! Satan, thou knowest thy kingdom is being shaken, and to-night thou hast lost a subject. ... O Church of the first-born in heaven! Admit me, Jesus, to be a member of it. ... Satan, thou art hanging on long, for thou hast had a strong hold here. Thou didst reign here even from infancy. Oh that thou wert dethroned in my heart! for thou hast swayed me too long. Jesus, Thou didst conquer on Calvary, come and save me! ... I come to Thee as a sinner, that I may be saved. I have nothing to give Thee in return but a broken heart. And, oh! it is hard, for it was long subject to Satan. Do Thou soften it. ... Oh, sin! sin! sin! thy weight is very heavy. ... Oh, the mountain is very high, wash it away!—it is very lofty, cast it behind Thee! ... Oh, this wounded soul! ... Light, light! ... I see faith coming under the door. ... I see the red river of Emmanuel's blood. I see the eternal river that flows from the side of Jesus. ... I see the top of the mountain is gone! Blessed Jesus! Thou hast begun a work. I trust to Thy name Thou wilt carry it on till our feet shall stand in the streets of the new Jerusalem. "Heaven and earth shall pass away, but Thy word shall never pass away."'

"These are but fragments," adds Mr Henderson, "of the prayer; but truly the kingdom of heaven suffered violence that night, and the violent took it by force. None that witnessed that spiritual conflict will ever forget it. What a reality it imparted to the solemn truths of God's Word, which, from our very familiarity with them, we too often fail to realise to their full extent!

THE PATHOLOGICAL AFFECTIONS

I should say that the young man who was the subject of this remarkable work had received nothing more than the rudiments of an English education. He had been a moral living youth, and a regular attender at the Sabbath-school and at public worship. Naturally he is of a retiring disposition, and not till this occasion had he ever offered a word of prayer before others. He would have been ashamed to have spoken of Jesus. I found, in conversation with him afterwards, that his mind was fully conscious during the great struggle through which he passed. There have been cases in which prayers were uttered by persons when under prostration, and were not remembered by them. It was different with him. He was never unconscious of anything that passed. The ministers present spoke to him at intervals, mentioning suitable texts of Scripture, and these his soul grasped at with wonderful avidity, and he would say, ' That is a promise. Oh, the sweet promises of God! Oh for faith to rest upon them!' At other times prayer was made for him, and he seemed to be encouraged thereby, as he exclaimed, ' Thou wilt hear the prayers of Thy faithful servants.' He mentioned to me afterwards, that when on his knees at prayer, the thought rushed into his mind that the moment of his salvation had come, and that it should be ' now or never.' It is interesting to know that his mother had experienced the blessed change the preceding night, and when he spoke to me some days afterwards of God's mercy towards him, he exclaimed, with streaming eyes, ' Ah, my mother was praying for me!' At the same time he thanked God for the Sabbath-school. ' Oh, blessed Sabbath-school, how much do I owe to you!'"

19

The Revival and its Lessons

To the record presented in the preceding pages it cannot be necessary to append any corroboration. Authenticated as the great awakening of 1859 has been by those who from the outset had the most abundant opportunities of estimating its real character and results, nothing further can be requisite to commend it as a genuine and wonderful work of God. Its origin and progress unequivocally attest it as divine. In startling and impressive grandeur it burst forth in a comparatively sequestered region, and scarcely had the new-born flame, drawn down by the few earnest watchers there, begun to burn than it spread in all directions over an entire province. All classes and all ages caught the heavenly fire. Within the Church a cold formality, an apathetic and unimpressible decorum were exchanged for a living and vigorous piety; without, the ignorant and unreclaimed were seized as by a resistless power; and from the ranks of the abandoned and the profligate, as well as of those who had been brought up under the droppings of the sanctuary, thousands and tens of thousands were made to realise the possession of an endless life.

In reviewing the course of this great spiritual movement as here narrated, there are many reflections which cannot but suggest themselves, which it must suffice only to mention.

I. Is not a narrative like the present fitted in an

REVIVAL LESSONS

eminent degree to revive the faith of the Church in the *omnipotent grace and energy of the Holy Spirit?*

II. What an illustration is presented by such a movement of *the rapidity with which God can bring about*, in accordance with the sure word of prophecy, *His purposes of mercy to the world!*

III. In contemplating the present awakening, it is interesting to observe the *marked coincidence between its leading features aud those which characterised the working of the Spirit in apostolic times.* (*Cf.* Acts ii. 42 *ff.*)

1. What *holding fast of the Christian profession!*
2. What steadfastness "*in doctrine!*"
3. What steadfastness "*in fellowship!*"
4. What inexpressible delight in *the* "*breaking of bread!*"
5. What continuance "*in prayer!*"
6. Of the "*fear that fell on every soul*" wherever this visitation came, innumerable instances are noticed in the preceding pages.
7. What a *oneness of interest* among the subjects of the awakening! even as when in the early time "all that believed were together, and had all things in common."

IV. May we not learn from such awakenings that for the conversion of the world *we do not need another gospel*, and *that the forces which the Church possesses*, always including, over and above mere machinery, the presence of the life-giving Spirit, *are amply sufficient for the great ends of her existence?*

V. We learn from such a work of grace as that which has taken place in Ulster, *the true theory and solution of the problem of Christian union*.

VI. This great awakening casts a new light upon the *duties and responsibilities of individual Christians*.

"'Thy kingdom come.' 'Even so, come, Lord Jesus!'"

APPENDIX

A. THE REVIVAL AND PUBLIC MORALITY

An attempt has been made in certain hostile quarters to depreciate the character of the revival by statistical statements affecting the moral status of Belfast. It has been alleged, for example, that drunkenness has been considerably on the increase since the commencement of the movement in that town. Before adverting more particularly to this representation, I may give a few detailed statistics in relation to crime in the province of Ulster during the year of the revival.

The number of prisoners for trial at the Quarter-Sessions for County Antrim, October 1859—that is, six months after the commencement of the revival—was exactly one-half that of the previous year; the figures being, October 1858—14; October 1859—7.

At the Ballymena Quarter-Sessions, held before John H. Otway, Esq., Assistant-Barrister, in April 1860,—that is, when the revival had been above a year in existence in that neighbourhood, which has been its central district,—*there was not a single case of indictment upon the record.*

On this subject, the following extract from a letter to the Bishop of Down from the Rev. Edward Maguire, the incumbent there, is valuable:—

"I met, a few evenings ago, a number of gentlemen connected with this neighbourhood. Among them there were three magistrates. Their unanimous testimony was, that since the revival the public morals were vastly improved; and though, as we might expect, there were some cases of drunkenness and other vices, yet they said these were quite exceptional. I asked various and independent parties,—the barrister (Mr Otway), magistrates, and grand-jurymen, all at different times and in different places,—to what cause, in their opinion, was this absence of crime owing, and they each and all at once replied, 'To the revival.'"

At the Quarter-Sessions in Coleraine, a place which is second in interest only to Ballymena, as one of the earliest scenes of the revival, the testimony of the assistant-barrister, to the same effect as given in the preceding part of this volume, was voluntarily emitted in presence of the grand jury.

At the Quarter-Sessions, Belfast, in April 1860, the assistant-barrister, as reported in the local journals, said, "I have been enabled, in the *first two towns* of the county in which I held the Sessions, to congratulate the grand jury upon having *nothing at all to do*. Gentlemen, I cannot exactly offer to you the same amount of congratulation, because you have *three cases* to try; but still I think we can congratulate ourselves on having such a small calendar, all of a *trifling character*."

At the March Assizes, 1860, for the county of Antrim, there were but five prisoners for trial; and for the county of the town of Carrickfergus, none.

APPENDIX

At the Quarter-Sessions for Londonderry, in April 1860, held before Wm. Armstrong, Esq., Assistant-Barrister, *there was no criminal business*, and his worship was presented with a pair of white gloves.

At the Spring Assizes for County Derry only three persons professing Presbyterianism were convicted.

An official connected with the county prison of Down says, in a private letter, "As to the criminal business of the county, the late Assizes (March 1860) had an average amount; but at the Quarter-Sessions, on several occasions, not a prisoner for trial appeared on the calendar, though some were out on bail."

One of the most important and decisive facts—as illustrating the moral results of the revival over the face of a whole county—is the following:—The number of committals for the county of Antrim had decreased from 3281 in 1858, to 2784 in 1859! It is well known that Antrim is predominantly Protestant in its population; yet the Protestants committed during the past year were only 1002, while the Roman Catholics were 1069, exhibiting a decrease of 99 Protestants as compared with the previous year, and an increase of 53 Roman Catholics.

In the County Monaghan prison, there is at present only a solitary Presbyterian—a respectable woman in humble life, whose mind gave way during the revival.

These are a few facts which are undisputed, and they ought to go far, even were there no other testimony, to settle the question of the moral tendencies and results of the revival.

A leading newspaper in Ulster, however, has attempted to show that, so far from promoting morality, the revival has actually fostered crime and increased immorality. The charge is serious; but what is its exact extent? It is stated, on the authority of certain police statistics, that drunkenness had increased during the year of revival beyond the proportion of ante-revival years. The cases were,—for 1858, 2539; for 1859, 3112—increase, 573. But the question arises, What have these statistics of drunkenness to do with the revival? Might it not be as well and as wisely said that drunkenness caused the revival, as that the revival caused drunkenness? The two things lie contemporaneously within certain months, but it is a logical fallacy to represent them as connected by relations so intimate as those of cause and effect. If it had been asserted by the advocates of the religious movement, that every individual of the 120,000 or 130,000 inhabitants of Belfast had been brought under the influence of the revival, these statistics of drunkenness might be legitimately appealed to in the case. But it is a fact which admits of no dispute that *no person has, during the year in question, been before the police court of Belfast, on a charge of drunkenness, who had ever been brought under religious influences*. According to the logic of this objector, the towns of Ballymena and Coleraine ought to be the most immoral and drunken in Ireland.

With regard to the increase of drunkenness in Belfast—as indicated by the police statistics—I do not see that the friends of the revival are under any obligation to account for them. It is well known, however, that the majority of the "drunken" cases are persons who make no profession of any form of Protestantism, and who constitute the lower *stratum* of the population of Belfast. There is reason, indeed, to believe that the immense majority of them are nominally Roman Catholics, who constitute about one-third of the inhabitants. It is further to be observed that in the cases above reported the same parties have in many instances been committed over and over again for the same offence. To whatever denomination they belong, they are of that degraded and criminal class which in our large towns and cities has never yet been reached by any of the appliances of evangelisation.

It is gratifying to state that Ballymacarrett, an almost exclusively Protestant suburb of Belfast, containing about ten thousand inhabitants, is undistinguished by this disgraceful inebriety. The police-books of Belfast testify that from Friday morning, 23rd December 1859, till Wednesday, the 28th of that month, including the Christmas holidays, only *three* persons were taken into custody in that whole district.

B. THE REVIVAL AND INSANITY

Akin to the charge just adverted to is the averment which has been put forward that the revival has promoted insanity to a degree fearfully in excess of all ordinary averages. The most exaggerated representations have been published on the subject, and have been caught up with great eagerness, and reproduced in the leading Popish, Tractarian, and anti-Evangelical journals of Britain.

It was stated, for example, in a Belfast journal, that "seven individuals had been admitted into the Belfast Lunatic Asylum within the last two weeks, whose aberration of mind is distinctly traceable to the excitement consequent on the religious preachings!"—(July 12, 1859). An inquiry was immediately instituted into the truth of this statement, when it appeared that two of the "cases" were women who had been in the asylum before, and had relapsed into insanity from the effects of the religious excitement; a male patient had been ill since the previous November—several months before the revival commenced—and no allegation was made at the time of his admission that he had come within reach of the revival excitement; another male patient was found to be afflicted with "acute mania"—quite a different thing from religious insanity; a female patient, admitted during the time specified, had been present at a revival meeting, where a woman seated near her was prostrated, but she herself had not fallen. No account has been given of the seventh case.

In the month of September 1859, the same journal published a paragraph, headed, "Insanity of Revivalism," which was to the following effect:—" We have it on good authority that, since the commencement of the revival movement, there have been lodged, in the Belfast Asylum and county jail no fewer than twenty-two cases of insanity from Larne and that neighbourhood alone." This was an astounding allegation, but it was promptly met by the following statement of facts:—As regards the Belfast Lunatic Asylum, only ONE case of insanity "from

APPENDIX

Larne and that neighbourhood alone" had been admitted, but it was a transfer from the county jail; so that, in reality, the Lunatic Asylum had none at all to account for. As regards the county jail, there were admitted, since the commencement of the revival, only five insane persons from Larne and its neighbourhood whose aberration was attributed to religious excitement. The precise nature of this aberration—as connected with religious excitement—is not stated in any document, and may have been wholly unconnected with the revival for aught that is shown. Of these five persons, one, as I have said, was transferred to the Lunatic Asylum, three had recovered, and one was still in the county jail on the 15th of September 1859.

I have obtained from an official connected with the Belfast Lunatic Asylum a list of all the cases admitted into that institution, classed under the head of religious excitement, during the year ended March 31, 1860. They are exactly sixteen, and include, of course, nearly all the cases already referred to. My obliging informant says in regard to these sixteen cases:—"You will perceive that a number of these cases come from jail, and in all such the particulars we receive are very imperfect. Several others, I believe, are represented very much according to the feeling of the medical man who visits the patient before admission, and it is he who gives the character to the disease, stating in his certificate the species of insanity with which the patient is afflicted. *I may mention that there were eight cases admitted here last year under the head of religious excitement, before there was any talk of revivals in the country.*" It follows, from this statement, that as there were sixteen cases in all, during the official year, only eight cases can be fairly attributed to the excitement of the revival—and this proportion is not in excess of the ordinary average!

So much for the cases in the Belfast Asylum. In that of Armagh, which was erected for the three counties of Armagh, Monaghan, and Cavan, there were only nine cases admitted last year whose insanity was traced to religious excitement; of these, six were discharged cured, and three relieved.

I believe that we should have heard little of the "insanity caused by the revival" had it not been for two or three melancholy cases, in which the religious excitement led to great physical exhaustion, and ultimately to untimely death. I am somewhat surprised, indeed, that there were not more of this description; for individuals were often in the habit of sitting up, night after night, engaged in religious exercises, and in a heated atmosphere, in defiance of all the laws of health; and it was not to be expected that, in the case of persons of morbid temperament, or predisposed to insanity, the exhaustion of nature, and the operation of moral causes of highly-wrought intensity, should not lead to mental derangement. Still, it is important to remark that all great crises in the history of the world, political as well as religious, have swelled the numbers of the insane; and I believe that the revival in Ulster has led to fewer instances of the kind than any similar movement on record. Sir Alexander Morrison, late physician to Bethlem Hospital, says:—"The predominant ideas of the times, whether religious or political, have great influence in the production of insanity. Thus, at the time of the Crusades, many cases of disordered mind occurred. The celebrated novel of Cervantes was written expressly to ridicule the insanity of knight-errantry prevalent about the time he wrote. *There were also, it is said, many persons afflicted with religious insanity at the time of the Reformation.*" I am not aware, however, that any section of the anti-Evangelical press has opposed or condemned the Reformation on the same ground as that on which the Ulster revival has been so unscrupulously vilified.

C. CONGREGATIONAL RETURNS

The following tabular statement contains the substance of returns from three hundred and seven out of four hundred and sixty Ulster congregations in connection with the General Assembly (there are five hundred and twenty in all, North and South), in reply to a circular issued in the month of December last. At that period, in most of the congregations referred to, there had been only one communion season subsequent to the revival. In such cases the returns do not by any means show the full extent of increase to the membership of the Church consequent upon the movement. In a few instances only, in which an unusually large accession is recorded, as in some of the Belfast congregations, the additions to the Church are reckoned up to the 1st of April 1860. The names of some congregations are reluctantly omitted, no definite numbers being specified in the returns received from them.

With reference to the cases of individuals formerly connected with the Roman Catholic Church, of which between three and four hundred are reported, it is to be observed that none are given but those of which a hopeful opinion is entertained in the several neighbourhoods with which they are connected.

The following abstract shows the comparative number both of congregations visited by the revival and of individuals added to the Church in the several counties of Ulster :—

	Congregations.	Additional Communicants.
Antrim,	81	4353
Down,	69	2132
Derry,	36	1258
Tyrone,	42	1189
Armagh,	27	625
Donegal,	23	502
Monaghan,	18	412
Cavan,	10	169
Fermanagh,	1	21
	307	10,661

In all the congregations throughout the Church, many who cannot be reckoned in the above statement, inasmuch as they were nominally in communion, have, after a long neglect, been reunited in the fellowship of the Church. The increase above the average, frequently stated below, is largely to be attributed to the accessions from this class, and amounts to several thousands.